PRAYING
IN HIS PRESENCE

PRAYING IN HIS PRESENCE

This book also has a companion recording. It includes prayers from the Psalms, spoken over instrumental music, and interwoven with songs. The resulting fabric of styles and sounds offers both musical appeal and devotional impact.

This Crystal Sea Book and its Crystal Sea Recording hold a unique relationship. The two need not be used together, nor are they dependent on each other. They are not simply printed and recorded versions of the same material. Instead, each supplements and enhances the other, using its own medium to accomplish the same goal: to draw the user into a spirit of prayer. Start with either the book or the recording, then you can move to the other for an enriching devotional experience.

The recording was produced by Steven V. Taylor, with concept and script created by Ken Bible.

Cassette	TA-4008C
Compact Disc	DC-4008

PRAYING IN HIS PRESENCE

Enjoying Constant Communication with God

❖

Devotional Readings by

KEN BIBLE

❖

CRYSTAL SEA
B O O K S

Kansas City, MO 64141

Copyright © 1993 by Ken Bible. All rights reserved.

Published by Crystal Sea Books, a division of Lillenas Publishing Company, Kansas City, MO 64141. Printed in the United States of America.

Cover Design: Paul Franitza

Unless otherwise indicated, all Scripture quotations are from the *Holy Bible, New International Version*® (NIV®). Copyright © 1973, 1978, 1984 by International Bible Society. Used by permission of Zondervan Publishing House. All rights reserved.

Quotations from the following Scripture versions are used by permission:

The *New American Standard Bible* (NASB), © The Lockman Foundation, 1960, 1962, 1963, 1968, 1971, 1972, 1973, 1975, 1977.

The *New Revised Standard Version* (NRSV), copyright © 1989, by the Division of Christian Education of the National Council of Churches of Christ in the United States of America.

To my wife,
Gloria

About
Praying in His Presence

This is not a how-to book on prayer. Neither does it discuss prayer in abstract terms. Instead, it seeks to draw the reader into a life of prayer—constant, personal prayer to the God who is constantly, personally with us. The meditations and prayer responses encourage simple, natural prayer. Each chapter relates such prayer to a different area of daily life.

Each chapter begins with a hymn that summarizes the main ideas of that chapter. You may choose to simply read each hymn as a devotional prayer. Or, if you care to sing the hymns, the name of an appropriate tune is given. These hymn tunes are chosen for their familiarity and may be found in nearly any hymnal (including the *Sing to the Lord* hymnal available from the publisher). Singing these opening hymns is one highly effective way to plant the truths in your mind and heart.

This book functions as a sequel to the volume *His Personal Presence*. However, *Praying in His Presence* also stands alone.

Each of these selections has grown out of my own experiences. Be encouraged! If the Lord can begin an effective and satisfying prayer life in me, with my wandering mind and short attention span, He can do it in you! And He will start right now if You simply turn to Him.

—KEN BIBLE

Contents

1

I LOOK TO YOU, LORD, IN YOUR PRESENCE

The Lord is near to all who call on him.
PSALM 145:18

EVER STANDING IN YOUR PRESENCE

Hymn

Ever standing in Your presence,
Ever living face to face,
Ever sharing, ever listening,
Ever open to Your grace.

> Refrain:
> *It's so good to just be near You,*
> *Free to bring You each request,*
> *Simply trusting You as Father,*
> *Free to serve and free to rest.*

Ever weak and ever needy,
Ever hungry for Your best,
Ever clinging to Your mercy,
Ever empty, ever blessed.

> Refrain:
> *It's so good to just be near You,*
> *Free to bring You each request,*
> *Simply trusting You as Father,*
> *Free to serve and free to rest.*

*This piece may be read as a devotional prayer, or may be sung as a hymn to the tune SATISFIED, "All My Lifelong I Had Panted."

Copyright © 1993 by Pilot Point Music. All rights reserved. Administered by Integrated Copyright Group, Inc., P.O. Box 24149, Nashville, TN 37202.

This hymn may be photocopied for noncommercial use by churches or groups that have a blanket license from Christian Copyright Licensing Inc. (CCLI), 6130 N.E. 78th Ct., Suite C-11, Portland, OR 97218-2853; 1-800-234-2446. For any other uses, contact Integrated Copyright Group at the address above.

Ever drawing us to know You,
Ever teaching to depend,
Ever loving, ever giving,
Ever God and ever Friend!

> *Refrain:*
> *It's so good to just be near You,*
> *Free to bring You each request,*
> *Simply trusting You as Father,*
> *Free to serve and free to rest.*
> —Ken Bible

❖

Natural Prayer

Meditation

Blessed are those . . . who walk in the light of your presence, O Lord.

They rejoice in your name all day long; . . . For you are their glory and strength (Psalm 89:15-17).

For YEARS I experienced a sense of uneasiness before God. I guess I felt I wasn't totally pleasing to Him, so I avoided looking in His face. I wanted to live closer to Him, and even believed that was possible, but I didn't know how to make it happen. Consistency was always beyond my reach.

I tried self-discipline. My time was organized into tight compartments, and I drove myself to stick to the program. And in the area of temptation, after my frequent failures, I would work out mental techniques to help me gain control the next time it came up. But all I tried only increased my frustration.

Nowhere was self-discipline a greater failure than in my prayer life. Yes, I understood the importance of praying, but that only made me feel more guilty. It wasn't just a matter of making time to pray. Once I started to pray, I couldn't concentrate to save my life. The harder I tried to control my wandering mind, the more it escaped in 80 directions.

And I studied the Bible. I studied it a lot. I guess I hoped the secret to a truly satisfying life in God was in some hidden wisdom He would help me find.

However, He graciously showed me the opposite. The key to the life He offers us is not through strict self-discipline, even though discipline can be good; nor is it through some higher wisdom attainable only by the spiritual elite. All He asks us to do—all He has ever wanted us to do—is to simply trust Him, one moment at a time. As we trust Him, a relationship is formed, a friendship that allows Him to live and work inside us.

Furthermore, He does not ask us to reach out to some God who is high above and far away. God is a real being, and He is constantly, personally with us.

Nothing has made a bigger difference in my spiritual life than that simple realization. I walk in His presence. I live with Him face to face.

"Faith" is now a deep, personal trust. Living a holy life flows from my relationship with Him as I let Him shape and guide me from the inside. And *He* is my joy. He himself. And He is my hope. I'm not talking about hope in some grand, "some day" sense. I refer to the hope that motivates us moment by moment, that drives our daily desires and expectations. He himself is that hope.

And He is my peace. Knowing I live in His presence makes each problem seem manageable.

But His constant presence makes the greatest change in my prayer life. No longer is prayer a routine of struggling to contact Someone way out there somewhere. No longer must I concentrate and try to force myself into the right frame of mind to pray. No longer is prayer a brief, isolated period of the day. It is wonderful to be able to:

Pray continually (1 Thessalonians 5:17).

We are never out of His presence, so prayer doesn't have to start and stop. He is always there, so we can talk to Him freely, moment by moment, as to a good friend who is right next to us. When He blesses us—through one of those little daily blessings—we can thank and praise Him on the spot. When a concern arises, we can talk to Him about it immediately. We can look in His face and know He loves us. We can trust the need to Him. Every joy, every problem, every gift from Him can become the seed of a prayer, of a nearer and dearer relationship with Him.

And when we fail, we can ask His forgiveness right there and then, knowing His love for us makes Him anxious to heal and forget completely. If our repentance is immediate and sincere, not even our sins need separate us from Him.

As our needs don't stop, prayer shouldn't stop. We can experience a continual openness, a quickness to turn to Him in everything. It won't happen automatically or overnight, but as we remember that He is there, and as we trust Him, our friendship grows. When it finally sinks in to you personally that He really is there with you, anxious to listen, anxious to guide and help you, prayer will become more natural and free. It will be a "want to," not a "have to."

Remember: always, always talk to Him as to a friend who is right there with you.

Move In, Lord

Prayer Response

Father, I spend most of my life
    alone with my own thoughts.
Invade those times, my Lord.
Move in and make them our times.

Dependent on Prayer

Meditation

I have set the LORD always before me. . . . There-
fore my heart is glad and my tongue rejoices; my
body also will rest secure (Psalm 16:8-9).

I CAN'T DESCRIBE how exciting and satisfying it is to
discover Christ as a real Being, One who is always with
me and in me. He is taking a more and more active role
in my daily life—the Lord is teaching me to depend on
Him more constantly and more practically in all I do.
I'm learning to turn my time over to Him, letting Him direct my schedule. I'm learning I can look to Him for
guidance and enabling in all my responsibilities, resting
in Him to accomplish through me all that needs to be
accomplished.

Having started to experience this way of living and
serving, I want so much to be this way only and always.
It's wonderful—more productive, more fulfilling, and
more natural. God is becoming more real and dear than
ever.

But I'm also finding that, accordingly, prayer is
more essential. *Depending on God is dependent on*
prayer. Prayer is the very breath of the relationship. In

daily life, with so much pressing us and distracting us, prayer is necessary to keep our hearts and minds turned to Him. We must bring our needs constantly to Him, remaining open to His influence and prompting.

I'm not talking about spending huge chunks of time locked in a room, trying to keep our minds on praying. Believe me, if that were what it took, I'd be lost. But I'm finding I need a heart given to prayer on a constant basis, learning to turn to Him quickly, moment by moment, in petition and thanksgiving, looking to Him for guidance in everything I face.

As with human families and friendships, communication is a key to a more satisfying relationship. To improve a relationship, we must improve the communication. We must make it more open, more constant.

To get a feeling for such openness, read about Christ in the Gospels. You get a sense of that unbroken communication between the Father and Jesus. Jesus seems to be always listening, always aware of His Father's presence and power. You can almost feel the bond of trust between them.

That's the kind of praying heart He wants us to have. His love wants that kind of relationship with us. And having just begun to taste such a life, that's what I want as well.

The Music of Prayer

Prayer Response

Lord, as I become more and more
    aware of Your presence,
Fill my life with the music of prayer,
    with the joy of being with You,
    with the desire to share in all You are.
Fill my heart with Yourself, my Lord.

The Simplicity of Love

Meditation

LISTEN to what the apostle Paul told the church at Corinth:

> *I am jealous for you with God's own jealousy, for I promised you in marriage to one husband, to present you as a pure virgin to Christ. But I fear that as the serpent deceived Eve by his cunning, your thoughts might be led astray from a simplicity toward Christ* (2 Corinthians 11:2-3, author's translation).

We are engaged to Christ, and we need to hold onto the simplicity of that relationship.

Most Bible versions translate that last phrase as "sincerity of devotion to Christ," but a more literal translation seems to be "simplicity toward Christ." I was drawn to that word "simplicity" because, at times, my Christianity seems anything but simple. Sometimes it seems fuzzy and distant and strained. I'm not sure what exactly is expected of me, nor how to accomplish it. And I guess I'm not sure what God really thinks of me with all my failures.

The original word translated "simplicity" here is rather interesting. In our culture, "simplicity" often holds negative connotations. To us, something "simple" is so elementary it's not worth our attention. Or, we are suspicious of anything too "simple," afraid it doesn't consider all the facts.

But the Bible talks about simplicity in a positive manner. It suggests a singleness of mind and heart, a freedom from pretense or divided loyalties. At times, "purity" is meant. That is the case in this passage, where Paul refers to the faithfulness of a bride to her husband. At other times, "sincerity" fits well, such as:

Slaves, obey your earthly masters in everything;
and do it, not only when their eye is on you and
to win their favor, but with <u>sincerity</u> of heart
(Colossians 3:22, emphasis added).

When connected with financial giving, it is translated "generosity." We're urged to give with a "singleness" or "simplicity" that gives openly, holding nothing back. After all, that's the way God gives to us (see James 1:5).

But with all the varied meanings, the one word that summarizes it for me is "wholeheartedness." This means having one purpose and one loyalty. This singleness of mind expresses itself in openhanded generosity and undistracted devotion.

Notice in the opening scripture that this undistracted devotion comes from an intimate, face-to-face love. It is like the wholeheartedness of a marriage engagement.

If you're married, do you remember your engagement? Spending time together, sharing feelings and concerns, expressing genuine love, being totally faithful to each other—all those actions were so natural. You felt no strain, no obligation, no dry routine. You did all this because you simply enjoyed each other. You were in love.

And if you'll reflect on your early days with Christ, you'll remember that same warm, natural love.

Your relationship with Him can still be like this. Look to God, and rediscover how beautiful He is, and how wonderful He can be in Your daily life. Fall in love with Him all over again.

Never forget that being a Christian is nothing but the simplicity and wholeheartedness of a personal love relationship with Jesus Christ as a living, wonderful Being.

Face to Face

Prayer

Lord, I love You face to face,
Heart to heart, in Your embrace.
Lifted, Jesus, by Your grace
I love You face to face.

Lord, I serve You face to face,
Deed by deed, through all I say.
Loving those who come my way,
I'll serve You face to face.

Lord, I'll praise You face to face,
Fully, gladly, grace by grace.
Here and now is just a taste—
I'll praise You face to face.

Copyright © 1993 by Pilot Point Music. All rights reserved. Administered by Integrated Copyright Group, Inc., P.O. Box 24149, Nashville, TN 37202.

God Finds Joy in You

Meditation

Let us rejoice in our Maker . . . For the Lord takes delight in His people (Psalm 149:2, 4, para.).

IMAGINE FOR just a minute: get a mental image of human beings in their most primitive condition, without all the trappings of education, hygiene, and culture. I picture cavemen from old television movies. You may envision a friend or relative. But think of the human creature completely natural and unadorned, in its rawest form.

Now realize that God seeks union with that creature. Cleanliness may be next to godliness, but remember that many people who were strangers to deodorant have enjoyed intimate fellowship with Him. People with no education have known the Unknowable and shared His wisdom. And creatures that seem so rough and repulsive at times can fully please a holy God. His Spirit can fill and fellowship with our spirit—that spirit within us that is deeper and more basic than our thin layer of cultural training.

Imagine that a caveman, by simply trusting his Creator, can be fully like Christ.

Pondering that makes me realize how little we understand the kind of beings we are—how we were originally made, and how God sees us from His perspective.

It also makes me realize how deeply He understands us and loves us.

The Lord takes delight in His people (v. 4, para.).

The Lord takes delight in you.

Yes, we can be so unbeautiful. It's easy to feel that the constant flow of our failures and inconsistencies surely washes away any good standing we might have with Him. But our relationship is much more basic and stable than that. His love embraces us at a deeper level.

Put yourself in this picture:

The LORD your God is with you, . . . He will take great delight in you, he will quiet you with his love, he will rejoice over you with singing (Zephaniah 3:17).

As a bridegroom rejoices over his bride, so will your God rejoice over you (Isaiah 62:5).

God enjoys just being with you. He takes pleasure in your company, the way a bridegroom enjoys being near his bride.

Pray that way. Talk to Him as One who is delighted to hear from you, who longs to share your thoughts, who deeply loves the most basic "you."

I Quiet Myself in Your Love

Prayer Response

I am Your child,
And You are my Father.
 I quiet myself in Your love.
You are the Lord
Above every other.
 I quiet myself in Your love.

 You are the greatest, and I am the least.
 You are the joy that will never cease.
 Here in Your presence is perfect peace,
 And I quiet myself in Your love.

When I'm in pain,
You feel what I'm feeling.
 I quiet myself in Your love.
When I am weak,
You're power and healing.
 I quiet myself in Your love.

 You are the greatest, and I am the least.
 You are the joy that will never cease.
 Here in Your presence is perfect peace,
 And I quiet myself in Your love.

You are my hope,
My glory and treasure.
   I quiet myself in Your love.
Praise to You, God!
I'll sing it forever!
   I quiet myself in Your love.

   You are the greatest, and I am the least.
   You are the joy that will never cease.
   Here in Your presence is perfect peace,
   And I quiet myself in Your love.

Be Open with God

Meditation

I have loved you with an everlasting love; I have drawn you with loving-kindness (Jeremiah 31:3).

*W*HEN SOMETHING happens to seriously shake the confidence of my wife, Gloria, she immediately withdraws emotionally, hiding her feelings behind a wall of silence and shallow smiles. She is overwhelmed with fears about herself, so she instinctively protects herself from further pain. For a while, she will not share herself with me.

Those brief periods are among the most painful in my life. I am cut off emotionally from the one I love. I feel powerless to help her when she needs me the most. Praying for the Lord's guidance, I work on communicating with her until she begins to open up. When she does, there is at first an outpouring of pain, frustration, and anger. But I welcome it because it's honest and because it paves the way to closeness.

My wife's withdrawals stem from fear. Mine stem from getting preoccupied. My mind fills with my own thoughts and projects, and without even realizing it, I distance myself from her. She senses my withdrawal and waits patiently—or not so patiently—to regain my attention. She wants that connection. She wants to know the eyes of my heart are fixed on her, that I am sharing myself with her and that I am open to her sharing.

If we crave such openness with those we love, how do you think God feels toward us? He doesn't operate out of an emotional need He has, but out of a real, deep, and burning love. How do you think He feels when He sees us struggle with concerns and needs we have never shared with Him? How does He feel when we so seldom look to Him or turn our hearts toward Him?

He died willingly, gladly, for our sins. His forgiveness is total, immediate, and from the bottom of His heart, without any recrimination whatsoever. How then must He feel when we hesitate to simply come to Him and lay our sins and failures before Him?

Does God desire anything more than that constant closeness with us? He has eliminated all the barriers of time and distance: He is personally with us moment by moment. We were unworthy, but He has made us worthy, welcoming us warmly, with open arms.

You live every second of your life in His presence. Share yourself with Him. Treat Him like someone with whom you are deeply in love. Turn to Him immediately with every concern, every need, every joy. Nothing in life—nothing—matches the excitement of experiencing God responding to you and loving you and growing inside you.

With My Whole Heart

Prayer Response

With my whole heart I trust You.
With my whole heart I seek You.
With my whole heart I rest in You, my Lord,
    Loving Lord of all my heart.

With Your whole heart You love me.
With Your whole heart You forgive me.
With Your whole heart You lift me up, my Lord,
    Loving Lord of all my heart.

With my whole heart I love You.
With my whole heart I adore You.
With my whole heart I turn to You, my Lord,
    Loving Lord of all my heart.

Copyright © 1992 by Pilot Point Music. All rights reserved. Administered by Integrated Copyright Group, Inc., P.O. Box 24149, Nashville, TN 37202.

Coveting His Control

Meditation

This is what the LORD says—your Redeemer, the Holy One of Israel: "I am the LORD your God, who teaches you what is best for you, who directs you in the way you should go" (Isaiah 48:17).

*I*N THE FALL of 1989 I felt the Lord leading me to compile a book proposal with some sample pieces of my writing and submit them to a publisher. A few months later, the publisher enthusiastically purchased the project. In October 1990 I completed the manuscript—a few weeks before my deadline. It looked like everything was going smoothly.

But from that point, nothing went right. The publisher and I couldn't agree on the approach and format of the book. After unsuccessfully working on a compromise for 18 months, we agreed to part ways. I submitted the book project to several other publishers, only to have each one reject it.

This was extremely discouraging at times. If I hadn't been sure the project was the Lord's idea, I would have given up.

But as the last rejection letter trickled in, the Lord reminded me of a project I was developing for Crystal

Sea Recordings—a musical recording on the same theme as the book. At His direct prompting, I suggested that the book and the recording be released together. Using both music and the printed word would be a unique way to communicate the central message. Previously, I had neither foreseen nor considered this possibility. But it seemed right to all involved, and in March 1993 *His Personal Presence* and Crystal Sea Books were born. As I watch the book and recording start to touch lives, I know:

> *The LORD has done this, and it is marvelous in our eyes* (Psalm 118:23).

I learned much through that whole agonizing process, but most importantly, I experienced what God can do when He is in control, when He calls every shot. And having experienced that, I never want it any other way. I'm determined not to settle for anything less than His complete control in every task I face.

You don't have to settle for anything less than His guidance either. You don't have to make your own way in this world and just hope for the best. As a child of God and as His Spirit-filled servant, you can walk in the confidence that He will always give you all the guidance you will trust Him for.

Yes, it will involve discouragements, setbacks, lots of waiting, and some seemingly blind alleys. Just read what His servants in the Bible endured. But God is God, and He is willing to be God in every area of your life— from the routine to the large. And once you've experienced His marvelous leadership, you won't want it any other way.

I'm just realizing how many areas of my life I had shut Him out of. I guess I didn't really believe He would get involved, so I just wasn't listening. I'm finding that the physical noise around us isn't what blocks His voice—He usually doesn't speak audibly anyway. He speaks to our minds and hearts. That's where the "noise" drowns Him out. The deafening roar is that of our own desires and plans. Our hearts and minds are focused on our own intentions, on working things out our way, and not on Him and His direction. If we want to hear His guidance, we must quiet our hearts, release our own plans, and look to Him for His will.

And He will lead. He always wants the very best for us, and He is always present, ready to give it. It's great to find that we can relax in His presence. You won't need to strain to hear Him—He knows how to speak so that you will hear. Just hold loosely to your own plans and learn to look to Him in everything.

Control Completely, God

Prayer Response

Lord God, in the presence of Your wisdom
    I quiet myself.
In the face of Your greatness
    I humble myself.
Touched by Your love,
    I rest myself.

Control completely, God.
    My heart is waiting.

2

I LOOK TO YOU, LORD, IN MY NEED

The Lord is near. Do not be anxious about anything, but in everything, by prayer and petition, with thanksgiving, present your requests to God. And the peace of God, which transcends all understanding, will guard your hearts and your minds in Christ Jesus.

PHILIPPIANS 4:5-7

I CANNOT SEE THE LIGHT, MY LORD

*Hymn

I cannot see the light, my Lord;
I only feel the fear;
And yet I know that You are God
When nothing else is clear.

I have no strength to lift myself,
But Lord, I lift my need
And spread before You all my fears.
Come take my hand and lead.

When all my joys have turned to pain
And hopes have fallen through,
I raise my eyes and fix my heart:
My only hope is You.

My God, my God, my hope, my joy,
You're with me in this place!
So in Your presence, in Your peace,
I trust, rejoice, and wait.

—KEN BIBLE

*This may be read as a devotional prayer, or may be sung to the tune SOME SOUL, "Lord, Lay Some Soul upon My Heart."

Copyright © 1993 by Ken Bible. All rights reserved. Administered by Integrated Copyright Group, Inc., P.O. Box 24149, Nashville, TN 37202.

This hymn may be photocopied for noncommercial use by churches or groups that have a blanket license from Christian Copyright Licensing Inc. (CCLI), 6130 N.E. 78th Ct., Suite C-11, Portland, OR 97218-2853; 1-800-234-2446. For any other uses, contact Integrated Copyright Group at the address above.

The Struggle of Faith

Meditation

Fight the good fight of the faith (1 Timothy 6:12).

*R*EAD ACTS 7 sometime. As part of Stephen's defense before the Jewish rulers, he summarizes the whole story of God's mighty works from Abraham to David. When you survey this chapter, it's a beautiful picture of God's power and faithfulness. How fortunate those people were to have experienced God's working so directly and miraculously!

But look more closely at their lives. Viewed on a day-to-day basis, each had its share of setbacks, hardships, delays, and suffering. At times, they seemed to bounce from one trouble to another. Look at Abraham, for instance. God's whole promise to him was based on the birth of a son, but Isaac wasn't born until his old age.

Joseph was sold into slavery by his own brothers (who would have preferred to kill him) and was later thrown into prison on a false charge. He only rose to power through a famine that lasted seven long years.

At 80 years old, Moses got one of the toughest assignments imaginable: free an entire nation from slavery, then lead them across a vast desert to a distant "promised land." The stories continue through the Old and the New Testaments.

We can see how incredibly faithful God was. He didn't just deliver these people; He actually used their troubles to demonstrate His power and goodness. As we sympathize with how they must have felt during their tough times, we find ourselves cheering them on: "I know it looks bad now, but you should see what God is about to do!"

No matter how circumstances seemed around them, He taught them to keep looking to Him and trusting Him. That's all God ever asked.

And make no mistake: our lives will involve struggle as well. We will experience hardship and opposition. At times we will face long delays when God seems silent and uninvolved.

But remember, for the believer, *every struggle is a struggle of faith*. No matter what the difficulty seems to be, our challenge remains the same: to continue to look to Him and follow Him, step by step.

God will work in us and through us and above us.

My God will meet all your needs according to his glorious riches in Christ Jesus (Philippians 4:19).

We know that in all things God works for the good of those who love him, who have been called according to his purpose (Romans 8:28).

Do not be terrified; do not be discouraged, for the LORD your God will be with you wherever you go (Joshua 1:9).

He just asks us to continue to trust Him.

Don't be distracted from God by today's problems. Keep your heart fixed on His face, and bring Him each concern as it arises. He is still with you, working to show all those around you just how good and faithful and loving He can be!

Face to Face

Prayer Response

Lord, I trust You face to face,
Need by need and day by day.
When You seem so far away,
I'll trust You face to face.

Copyright © 1993 by Pilot Point Music. All rights reserved. Administered by Integrated Copyright Group, Inc., P.O. Box 24149, Nashville, TN 37202.

Nine Months Pregnant

Meditation

"Do I bring to the moment of birth and not give delivery?" says the LORD *(Isaiah 66:9).*

I REMEMBER when my wife, Gloria, was pregnant with Jason, our eldest child. As we attended childbirth classes, she felt the insecurities that I'm sure most mothers-to-be share: will I be able to do it? Will something go wrong? And even though I was only a coach and hand-holder, I too was apprehensive about the whole process.

I remember the teacher repeating to the class the same basic assurances over and over: childbirth is a natural function, and one way or another, the baby will be born. Unless you've been through it, that probably sounds laughable. But during the long months of waiting and wondering, we clung to those statements. And even when the day came, as Gloria's intense pain gnawed relentlessly, and the hospital staff seemed so unhurried—we wondered if the delivery would ever really happen.

At one point in my life, I had to cling to those assurances for eight long years. All my adult life, I had felt the call and the drive to be a writer. And though I had written a few song lyrics and articles, I seemed powerless to really pursue it. My busy schedule and caring for my family prevented the necessary time to devote to it. I had an immediate call from God to teach Bible studies—a responsibility that fed my desire to write but also squeezed it out of my schedule.

Besides, I had a job as director of Lillenas Publishing Company, a major church music publisher. I knew the Lord had placed me in this job, and He abundantly blessed the company's efforts. But I was itching for a new challenge. To make matters much worse, as the company grew, so did my responsibilities. Unable to hire additional staff to lighten the load, I felt crushed.

I investigated every other line of work that seemed even remotely feasible. But as one door after another slammed in my face, I finally left the whole matter in the Lord's hands and continued where I was.

Eight years after my search for fulfillment began, the Lord moved. He led me into a new relationship with Lillenas. With shorter hours and fewer responsibilities, I had both the time to write at home and the freedom to develop some unique new products at Lillenas. This was the Lord's perfect will in His perfect timing, and the years since have been wonderful.

My experience is so common. Most of us endure times when, in some important area, we feel nine months pregnant, with discomfort and pressure that won't quit, but no relief in sight. We feel full term, but God is in no hurry.

During my "labor," Isaiah 66:9 gave me an assurance that helped me hold on. And I can testify that God never begins anything in our lives that He won't finish—beautifully, completely, and perfectly. All that His love has conceived, He will deliver, and at the right time.

If you're feeling nine months pregnant, learn to rest in Him more constantly and completely. He is drawing you to himself. Even as you wait, He is working all things for your good and for the blessing of those around you.

Now to him who is able to do immeasurably more than all we ask or imagine, according to his power that is at work within us, to him be glory . . . for ever and ever! Amen (Ephesians 3:20-21).

❖

Fulfill

Prayer Response

Fulfill in me
Your perfect will in me,
Creator wise
Whose loving eyes
Will never leave Your children.

Secure, I'll trust
My Father sure and just.
To run or rest,
You know what's best,
And I will gladly follow.

When Discouragements Come

Meditation

---

*O our God . . . we have no power . . . We do not
know what to do, but our eyes are upon you* (2
Chronicles 20:12).

*E*ACH OF OUR LIVES and our work has its own
share of discouragements. My work in the publishing
field is certainly no different. Though the last few years
have been the most satisfying in my life, I've also had
the most discouragements to deal with. However, prayer
has helped turn these setbacks into benefits in several
ways.

1. Discouragements force me to look to God and
seek His will for my life. First and foremost, I want to be
where He wants me to be, no matter how the situation
looks.

2. Once I know that God has led me to this point, I
can stand on that. I can rest in the fact that God always
finishes what He starts. When we invest our lives for the
Lord, we don't need to check the daily Dow-Jones aver-

ages. He's into long-term investments—but His yields are terrific. Feeding the 5,000 from a few loaves and fishes is not an isolated event with Him. Just look at your own life, and you'll doubtless see lots of times when He reaped a lot from a little. But this process often requires patience. Don't be distracted by the daily ups and downs. Focus on following Him, and trust Him for the harvest.

3. When things don't seem to be going right in my area of service to Him, I know I can't just pray out of selfish interest. Thus I'm forced to set aside my own ego and personal concerns. I must pray simply for what is best for His purposes and for the good of His people. I believe that's what is meant by praying "in His name." When we pray solely for the good of God's own work, having removed our own motivations, we can pray boldly and ask largely. Praying like this also helps focus our hearts on loving God's people and keeping their good in view.

4. When I get discouraged, I frequently find God reminding me that my work is not my joy: He himself is my joy. Being in His presence, knowing Him, sharing life personally with Him—*this* is my satisfaction and my reason for being. My heart and my hope are to center upon Him, not upon my work. God is a jealous God who wants our love personally. It's easy to let our service to Him become our focus, rather than making Him our focus, with our service being a natural outflow of our personal relationship. He desires that relationship more than any works we can do.

Disappointments can truly strengthen our trust in God, purify our motives, and recenter our hearts on Him alone.

Every Need a Seed of Prayer

Prayer Response

Father,
Let every need be a seed of prayer—
Each joy and hope, each fear and care.
In all I do, I'll look to You.
Lord, draw my heart to prayer.

Love That Teaches

Meditation

My son, do not make light of the Lord's discipline, and do not lose heart when he rebukes you, because the Lord disciplines those he loves, and he punishes everyone he accepts as a son. Endure hardship as discipline; God is treating you as sons. For what son is not disciplined by his father?

Moreover, we have all had human fathers who disciplined us and we respected them for it. How much more should we submit to the Father of our spirits and live! Our fathers disciplined us for a little while as they thought best; but God disciplines us for our good, that we may share in his holiness. No discipline seems pleasant at the time, but painful. Later on, however, it produces a harvest of righteousness and peace for those who have been trained by it (Hebrews 12:5-7, 9-11).

*F*ATHER" HAS GROWN to be the name for God that is most dear and meaningful to me. This personal name expresses intimacy and belonging. It reminds me of His deep love for me as His own son. And when I speak it to Him, the word says, "I love You and trust You and reverence you."

But the Scripture above adds a new side to this picture of God as my Father. It says that God disciplines ALL His children—including me.

Does that mean that God sends troubles our way? Or perhaps He just allows them, then uses them for our good? I won't attempt to answer those questions. My concern is what His discipline has to do with me.

I think of my three teenagers. The older they get, the more I realize they will only grasp many truths through personal experience. I can talk and talk, but some lessons will never penetrate their shells. Like all of us, they base their decisions on how they see the world. Unfortunately, there is so much of the world they haven't seen. But pain is a great teacher, and they will learn, just as we did.

I think of my own life. If I didn't experience all the tough times, how much would I really understand of God's tender, personal love for me? Would I realize that He cares about my finances, my car, my children, my job—everything I care about—and that He is willing to be involved in all those areas?

How often have I cried in desperation, "Lord, You are able—why don't You just take away these desires?" Yet without my shameful failures, would I grasp how constantly I need to depend on Him? Would I have tasted the depths of my own self-centeredness, the terrible bondage of sin, or the wonderful freedom of holiness? Could I have ever believed how incredibly merciful He is?

Without the demands of family life, would we ever understand the demands of love, or its blessings?

He has spoken so many truths to us in the Bible, and He has called us to simply trust Him. But these truths often don't come alive for us until we experience life's discipline.

Remember, God is not a scowling disciplinarian, standing over us with a switch in His hand. I hurt for people who travel through life with a guilt complex, thinking each new trouble is a punishment from God for some failure. Our Father is not like that. He is eager to teach us, eager to lift us and show us how deeply He cares. His heart is anxious to give us His very best, and not even the life of His only Son is too great a price to pay.

Trust Him. Look to Him in everything, and let each situation teach You more about His love for you.

All the ways of the LORD are loving and faithful
for those who keep the demands of his covenant
(Psalm 25:10).

Shape Me, Lord

Prayer Response

My Father,
I see You only dimly.
I see little of the needs around me,
    or of the depths of my own need.
I do not see what the future holds.
You see.
Shape me, Lord.

I am weak
    and selfish,
    inconsistent
    and shortsighted.
I know but do not do.
You are love.
Shape me, Lord.

You are Creator and Provider,
    Shepherd and Servant,
    Helper and Healer,
    Forgiver and Friend and Holy Father.
I want to be Your child.
Shape me, Lord.
Shape me.

Can I Trust God with My Car?

Meditation

Cast all your anxiety on him because he cares for you (1 Peter 5:7).

I HATE CARS. They're OK when they work fine, but when they don't, they make my stomach grind like nothing else can.

I'm tempted to launch into one of my car repair stories. But we could aggravate each other for hours with such tales. Suffice it to say that car repairs involve money, inconvenience, more money, more inconvenience, and trusting people we don't trust.

Through all this gnashing of teeth over cars, however, the Lord is teaching me valuable lessons. One is the blessing of living as His steward. When I depend on Him to provide all my needs, and when I am willing to spend my resources as He wants me to spend them, I can turn my car problems over to Him. "Lord, they want $280 to fix the car. It's Your money and Your car. I am just Your steward. Have Your will, Lord."

Does the Lord heal cars? I can only tell you that on a number of occasions, big repairs have turned into small repairs or have disappeared completely when I've left the matter with Him. And I can tell you that in every case, thinking and living as His steward brought me freedom and peace.

But to be honest, money isn't what upsets me most about car repairs. To get my car to a mechanic, I must forfeit a morning I would otherwise spend writing, and that bothers me more than the repair bill. But even with that, I can trust God and turn my schedule over to Him without too much wear and tear on my stomach.

I've discovered what really upsets me about car repairs is my feeling of helplessness and uncertainty. I don't understand cars. I don't know if the problem can be fixed. I don't know if I can trust the mechanic. When it comes to cars, I feel ill-at-ease and unsure of myself from beginning to end.

I suppose that's why I dread certain jobs at work—the ones in which I lack confidence or expertise. That's also why I hate returning phone calls: I don't know what demands await me on the other end. Feeling helpless and insecure is extremely uncomfortable, especially for one who is used to feeling in control.

And control is the real question, isn't it? Completely surrendering control to God is tough. We instinctively cling to it, as to survival itself. When we start to feel control slipping away from us, we become anxious, even frantic.

But circumstances sometimes arise that render us helpless, ripping control from our hands. If we then, in desperation, throw ourselves completely on God, we can experience how wonderful it is to live and rest in His control. And having tasted that freedom and rest, we want to trust Him more completely, and in more areas of our lives. We were meant to spend our lives resting in His hands.

Each new need—even a car problem—can become an opportunity to discover God, whose care is more practical and complete than we can imagine.

I Bring My Weakness to You

Prayer Response

Lord, I bring my car to You.
I bring my money to you, and all my possessions.
I bring my time and my schedule to you.
But most of all, I bring myself and all my weakness.
Take me, Lord.
I gladly give You control
    and rest in Your goodness.
I love You, my Father.

Financial Security

Meditation

Find rest . . . in God alone; . . . Though your riches increase, do not set your heart on them (Psalm 62:5, 10).

I SUPPOSE Gloria and I hope for the same benefits from our money that many of you want: comfort; security; the freedom to do what we'd like.

We've been blessed with relative financial stability during our marriage. Our income has never been high, but it's been steady. And though finances have been tight at times, we've never been in dire need. We've faced no major catastrophes.

But as with most people, our finances do seem to go in cycles. We experience waves of extra bills, then, on occasion, periods of extra income. Since surviving a number of these waves, I can look back and have some perspective on them. No matter how many extra bills have come in, we've always been able to pay them somehow, and in a reasonable amount of time.

On the other hand, the "extra" income is almost never extra. It is usually gobbled up rather quickly by more bills—either new purchases or maintenance on past purchases: house, appliances, car, or whatever. On rare occasions, we can add modest amounts to our savings, but not enough to bring any real security.

With all the concern we lavish on our finances, I've started viewing money as empty threats, empty promises. The bills have turned out to be less of a threat than we feared at times. And the extra income, on which we tend to focus so much hope, hasn't performed as anticipated. Empty threats, empty promises.

We want comfort, security, and freedom. But life's needs and insecurities run deeper than money could ever handle. Family relationships, job satisfaction, health—not to mention the health of our relationship with Christ—these are far more critical than money. And as to freedom, God seems to bring us life opportunities that are neither initiated nor limited by finances.

In other words, I'm discovering several basic truths about money. If I want comfort, security, and freedom:

1. Bills aren't the real enemy: anxiety about money is. That anxiety can flourish whether bills are high or income is high, and it destroys the sense of comfort, security, and freedom we seek.

2. Extra income isn't my real need: trusting God is. He really can deliver these wonderful blessings, and more.

I still catch myself wishing for more income. But what I really want is to keep our finances in His hands, whether the bills or the income seem to be running ahead at the moment. Having our finances in His hands brings satisfaction that income can't give and bills can't take away.

Rest

Prayer Response

> *Come to me, all you who are weary and burdened, and I will give you rest* (Matthew 11:28).

Father, I've turned everywhere else.
I've sought relaxation instead of rest.
I've substituted comfort for peace.
The shell of security I've tried to build
    only weighs me down with anxiety.

I hear Your words of love:
> *In quietness and trust is your strength* (Isaiah 30:15).

> *Take my yoke upon you and learn from me, for I am gentle and humble in heart, and you will find rest for your souls* (Matthew 11:29).

And God of fervent love,
    passionately jealous for my best good,
I turn to You now.
God, what if I could truly know You—
    not just know about You,
    but know *You?*
What if by simple trust I could realize
    Your personal presence with me,
    moment by moment?
If in that presence I could know
    Your gentleness,

Your power,
Your faithfulness,
Your love?
If trust could become
    a personal relationship between us,
    not an abstract concept?
What if I could simply know You,
    and know You always with me?

Would Your rest then reign in me?
Would it fill my mind, my emotions,
    and the desires of my heart?
Would it put me at peace with the past,
    at peace with the present,
    and eagerly anticipating
    a glorious future in You?
Would it reconcile me to myself,
    to each person in my life,
    and to You?
Could I go to bed in it,
    get up in it,
    work, have fun, and face adversity in it
    without getting it wrinkled?

Would I then share Your deep peace—
    that wholeness and harmony
    You enjoy within Yourself,
    that is found in You alone?

Come to me . . . and I will give you rest
(Matthew 11:28).

Father, I want to know You.
I want to live in Your presence.
I come to You now.

3

I LOOK TO YOU, LORD, IN MY STRUGGLE WITH SIN

Submit yourselves, then, to God. Resist the devil, and he will flee from you. Come near to God and he will come near to you.

JAMES 4:7-8

Who is a God like you, who pardons sin . . . ? You do not stay angry forever but delight to show mercy. You will again have compassion on us . . . and hurl our iniquities into the depths of the sea.

MICAH 7:18-19

To him who is able to keep you from falling and to present you before his glorious presence without fault and with great joy—to the only God our Savior be glory, majesty, power and authority . . . now and forevermore! Amen.

JUDE 24-25

FATHER, I'VE FAILED YOU

Hymn

Father, I've failed You.
See my sin and selfishness;
    See how I've nourished my foolish pride.
Touch with Your mercy;
Speak Your forgiveness
    Through all the guilt I've tried to hide.

Jesus, my Brother,
Human, Holy Savior,
    You feel the weakness I feel within.
You are my Righteousness;
You are my Confidence,
    For when I'm weak, Your strength begins.

Moment by moment,
Marvelous, Almighty God,
    Resting in You, I am truly free.
Teach me to trust You;
Teach me to walk in You,
    My Lord, my Strength, my Liberty!

—KEN BIBLE

*This may be read as a devotional prayer, or may be sung to the tune CRUSADERS' HYMN, "Fairest Lord Jesus."

Copyright © 1993 by Ken Bible. All rights reserved. Administered by Integrated Copyright Group, Inc., P.O. Box 24149, Nashville, TN 37202.

This hymn may be photocopied for noncommercial use by churches or groups that have a blanket license from Christian Copyright Licensing Inc. (CCLI), 6130 N.E. 78th Ct., Suite C-11, Portland, OR 97218-2853; 1-800-234-2446. For any other uses, contact Integrated Copyright Group at the address above.

God, My Brother

Meditation

Both the one who makes men holy and those who are made holy are of the same family. So Jesus is not ashamed to call them brothers. . . . He too shared in their humanity. . . . He had to be made like his brothers in every way (Hebrews 2:11, 14, 17).

*W*E TEND to think of God as being radically different from us, living in another realm. And in a sense, that's true.

But I'm startled to realize I can relate to God as a fellow human being. My emotions, my weaknesses, the drives I struggle to understand and control—He has lived through them all, day by day, just as I am doing. He doesn't understand humans in a detached sense. He is one. He knows exactly how we feel.

Because he himself suffered when he was tempted, he is able to help those who are being tempted (Hebrews 2:18).

Before I confide in someone, I want to be sure that person can understand what I'm experiencing. I need to know he'll be sympathetic. Otherwise I won't make myself vulnerable. When I'm hurting and ashamed, the last thing I want is a critical attitude staring back at me.

But I can be perfectly open with Jesus. He is my Brother, and I know He understands. I can be honest about all my personal problems, knowing that His only attitude toward me is love—always, only love.

More than that, He helps. Whenever I have looked to Him and trusted Him in times of temptation, He has always given me just the strength I need for that moment. And when I need guidance, He gladly gives it, Person to person.

We do not have a high priest who is unable to sympathize with our weaknesses, but we have one who has been tempted in every way, just as we are—yet was without sin. Let us then approach the throne of grace with confidence, so that we may receive mercy and find grace to help us in our time of need (Hebrews 4:15-16).

We can always come to Him with confidence. Do you realize how wonderful that is? No matter how small the dilemma, if you care, He cares. If you face a temptation you'd be ashamed to share with anyone, you can be open with Him and know He will understand and guide you through it.

And if you've sinned and are struggling with the guilt, you can still come to Him with confidence. Hard to believe, but true. If you'll trust Him, His forgiveness is immediate and completely free.

His compassions never fail. They are new every morning; great is your faithfulness (Lamentations 3:22-23).

He has broken down all the walls between Him and you—the walls of human weakness, of time and space, of all your sins and your guilt. You can look into His face, bringing Your temptations and Your failures, knowing He is mercy and strength and unbroken love.

Praise to You, Lord!

I Choose Your Presence

Prayer Response

Jesus—
Jesus—
My God,
My Brother—

In my helplessness and shame,
I open myself to You.
I lay myself completely on Your mercy.

And in the face of temptation,
By Your help this moment,
I choose the pleasure of Your presence.
I choose the pleasure of pleasing You.

I love You, my Lord.

*O God, you are my God, earnestly I seek you;
my soul thirsts for you . . . (Psalm 63:1).*

The Blind Man of Jericho

Meditation

As Jesus approached Jericho, a blind man was sitting by the roadside begging. When he heard the crowd going by, he asked what was happening. They told him, "Jesus of Nazareth is passing by."

He called out, "Jesus, Son of David, have mercy on me!"

Those who led the way rebuked him and told him to be quiet, but he shouted all the more, "Son of David, have mercy on me!"

Jesus stopped and ordered the man to be brought to him. When he came near, Jesus asked him, "What do you want me to do for you?"

"Lord, I want to see," he replied.

Jesus said to him, "Receive your sight; your faith has healed you." Immediately he received his sight and followed Jesus, praising God. When all the people saw it, they also praised God (Luke 18:35-43).

*J*ESUS' LIFE was filled with individual encounters. Sometimes these meetings were private, but more often they occurred during a busy day with crowds pushing all around.

The stories of these encounters are so familiar and the recorded portions of the conversations so brief that the words fly past us. We don't comprehend what really transpired in human terms. We often fail to understand the encounters on an emotional level.

Read the above story again. This time, enter into it. Try to hear what the participants heard and feel what they felt—the blind man, those leading the way, and Jesus.

What if you were blind, doomed to spend every day begging as life went on around you? But suddenly you learn your only hope for healing is passing nearby— right now, at this very moment.

Jesus . . . have mercy on me! (v. 38).

It was a cry of weakness and need, of complete helplessness. "Jesus, I'm desperate! Please notice me! Help me! Lord, care about me!"

Have you ever noticed what happens when someone speaks too loudly or has an emotional outburst that seems inappropriate? It disrupts decorum, and the whole atmosphere becomes tense. Everyone is suddenly uncomfortable—and annoyed.

Those who led the way rebuked him and told
him to be quiet (v. 39).

But he was desperate, so he yelled even louder and more insistently,

Son of David, have mercy on me! (v. 39).

This cry arose from the depths of his heart, all the way up through his being. Propriety, reputation, and embarrassment didn't matter. Nothing else mattered. He was in the presence of One who could give him his life. "Jesus—HELP ME!"

We can approach God like that man. All of us have felt some measure of what the blind man felt before God: crushing need, helplessness, desperation. When you feel that way, cry out to God. He is not offended by honesty, no matter how brutal. Read the Gospels. Read the Psalms. He honors faith.

Jesus said to him, "Receive your sight; your faith has healed you" (v. 42).

No poverty should make us too ashamed to come to God. Whether the need is moral or emotional, large or small, you are welcome in His presence. You are an invited guest. And He will look you straight in the eye, straight in the heart, and work in your life. He may not act according to your plan or on your timetable, but trust Him through your pain. His wisdom and love will prove themselves perfect.

He received his sight and followed Jesus, praising God. When all the people saw it, they also praised God (v. 43).

Out of the Depths

Prayer Response

Out of the depths I cry to you, O Lord;
O Lord, hear my voice.
Please listen to my cry for mercy.

If you kept a record of sins,
O Lord, who could stand before You?
But You are forgiving,
so I come.

I wait for You, Lord.
My soul waits,
and in Your word I put my hope.
My whole being waits for You
more than a weary watchman waits
for the morning.

O Lord, I trust You;
for Your love never fails.
You will deliver me completely
from all my sin.

Psalm 130, paraphrase

His Strength Through My Weakness

Meditation

There was given me a thorn in my flesh, a messenger of Satan, to torment me. Three times I pleaded with the Lord to take it away from me. But he said to me, "My grace is sufficient for you, for my power is made perfect in weakness." Therefore I will boast all the more gladly about my weaknesses, so that Christ's power may rest on me (2 Corinthians 12:7-9).

*H*AS SOME GUILT or failure plagued you repeatedly? Most of us believe Christ is faithful—if we repent, He forgives and enables us to be victorious over any weakness or temptation. But what do you do when you fail, repent sincerely, only to fail again, and again, and again?

Soon, frustration sets in. Then come the doubts. Every new failure mocks not only you and your commitment, but your faith in God.

If you have reached that point of feeling totally aggravated and helpless, try this: take that sense of helplessness to God. Sometimes the only fruit of years of struggling is an overwhelming realization that we are totally inadequate to handle our own weaknesses.

But that realization is a great gift, only a small step of faith away from freedom, joy, and power in Christ.

My grace is sufficient for you, for my power is made perfect in weakness (v. 9).

We instinctively try to deal with our weaknesses ourselves by struggling harder, or by stricter self-discipline, or by some technique or program. We attempt to make ourselves adequate. Only when any illusion of our own ability is shattered do we release control to Him. Only when our total helplessness overwhelms us do we simply lay ourselves on Him.

Remember: *you fail, not because you are weak—you will always be weak—but because you do not trust God in that weakness.*

If you're finally at the end of yourself, look to Him —and rejoice! He has brought you to a wonderful new beginning. You are ready for your first day in the school of dependence.

I Look to You in Temptation

Prayer Response

Father, when I handle temptation
    in my own strength,
The result is failure and frustration.
The harder I fight, the more entangled I get
In the web of my own weakness.

Teach me to do all I can to flee temptation,
But when it comes,
Let me hear it immediately as a call
To look to You,
To trust my needs to You,
To rest in You—
    My Father,
    My Creator,
    My Loving Savior.

Thank You, Lord.

Freedom

Meditation

Thanks be to God that, though you used to be slaves to sin. . . . you have been set free from sin and have become slaves to righteousness (Romans 6:17-18).

*I*F YOU HAVE struggled with a persistent sin for very long, you've probably reached the same conclusion I have: we cannot free ourselves from sin.

But I have great news: you *are* free.

We died to sin; how can we live in it any longer? . . . For we know that our old self was crucified with him so that the body of sin might be done away with, that we should no longer be slaves to sin . . . Count yourselves dead to sin but alive to God in Christ Jesus (Romans 6:2, 6, 11).

When we trusted Christ for our salvation, He forgave us and cleansed us and released us from Satan's power over us. He has given us the freedom to turn away from sin.

I had surrendered to temptation so many times that when it came, I felt powerless to resist it. How wonderful it was when God reminded me that He had freed me, and that the choice of whether to give into the temptation was mine.

Do not let sin reign in your mortal body so that you obey its evil desires. Do not offer the parts of your body to sin, as instruments of wickedness, but rather offer yourselves to God. . . . For sin shall not be your master (Romans 6:12-14).

God is faithful; he will not let you be tempted beyond what you can bear. But when you are tempted, he will also provide a way out so that you can stand up under it (1 Corinthians 10:13).

But if this is true, why do we continue to fail?

We fail when we fail to trust God. When temptation first whispers, stop and turn to Him. Commit those next few minutes to Him, as your Father, your Creator, and your Savior. Satan will try to distract you from God—either through the sin's attractiveness or through fear of its power over you. But each time temptation tugs, express that simple commitment again, giving Him those few moments. Remember:

Our needs come one at a time.

His grace comes one need at a time.

Trust Him for one grace at a time.

God is our only strength, and victory always comes through dependence on Him.

Living in Freedom

Prayer Response

Lord, I want to live in the freedom of
    Your love and Your power
    this moment.
I look to You and
    trust You and
    love You, my Father.

Fruits of Repentance

Meditation

> *Since we are surrounded by such a great cloud of witnesses, let us throw off everything that hinders and the sin that so easily entangles . . . Let us fix our eyes on Jesus, the author and perfecter of our faith* (Hebrews 12:1-2).

THROUGHOUT our Christian walk, Christ calls us out of destructive life-styles and toward himself. For many of us, responding to His call involves throwing off hurtful habits that have entangled us. While some seem instantaneously delivered from these habits, others must follow a process that can be frustrating and discouraging.

If you struggle with such a habit or with some recurring sin, this passage may prove helpful:

When crowds came to John to be baptized, he demanded that they

> *Produce fruit in keeping with repentance* (Luke 3:8).

Seekers from a variety of backgrounds wanted to know what this repentance demanded of them. They asked:

> *What should we do then?* (Luke 3:10).

John answered by spelling out specific life changes that each group needed to make. Those with plenty

were to share with the needy. Tax collectors were to col-
lect only the taxes the law required. Soldiers were told
not to extort money, not to make false accusations, and
to be content with their pay.

For all of us, repentance is more than words, no
matter how sincerely spoken. It is more than good intentions, no matter how pure and noble. If repentance is real, it will be accompanied by changes in the way we
live—changes that act out our desire to turn away from
sin forever. When our prayer is "lead us not into temptation" (Matthew 6:13), we will do all we can to avoid
that temptation.

If sin is a problem in your life, and if you deeply
long to break your cycle of failure, why not get in line
with the sinners, the soldiers, and the tax collectors?
Ask God with a sincere and open heart, "What fruits of
repentance would You have me produce, Lord? What
changes would You have me make to break my sinful
patterns?"

Listen, and I believe you'll get an answer tailored to
your need. The Savior will not ignore a seeking heart,
and His wisdom is extremely practical. He may ask you
to consciously avoid certain situations or to establish
more positive habits. He may want you to make yourself
accountable to a trusted Christian friend.

Whatever His response to you, write it down and
begin obeying Him. Remember, you live in His presence
every moment. Trust Him one step at a time, and He
himself will lead and enable and bless you.

What Is Hindering Me?

Prayer Response

Jesus, I fix my eyes on You.
What is hindering me
    from following You more boldly?
What is distracting me
    from hearing Your words more clearly?
What will I gladly throw aside
    after just one glimpse of eternity?

Speak, Lord;
Speak Your love,
And I will listen.

New Driver

Meditation

The LORD is compassionate and gracious, slow to anger, abounding in love. . . . He does not treat us as our sins deserve . . . For as high as the heavens are above the earth, so great is his love . . . As a father has compassion on his children, so the LORD has compassion on those who fear him; for he knows how we are formed, he remembers that we are dust (Psalm 103:8, 10-11, 13-14).

*M*Y SON is a new driver. He's rather confident in his new expertise, assured he can handle any situation (though he has no way of knowing what those situations will be). He's impatient with our parental concerns, eager for independence above all else. He says he can drive. The school says he can drive. The state says he can drive.

And he can drive, as long as it's smooth sailing. When situations are normal and all is clear, he's in control. But when the roads are crowded or unexpected demands are made, when quick thinking and experience are required, he bungles the basics. His reactions are not yet practiced or polished. His confidence suffers a sudden attack of realism, and he panics, takes chances, and sometimes uses poor judgment.

For example, on his first Sunday in the church parking lot, he turned the wrong way down a one-way aisle, went too fast trying to pull into a parking space slanted the opposite direction, and scraped the side of a car. $285 in cash (we decided not to bother the insurance company).

Still, he is on the road, risking the life and well-being of not only himself but all who cross his path—not to mention that he is a hazard to our pocketbook.

This helps me realize that to God, my Father, I must seem much like my son. I have so much experience as a Christian. I've studied and listened and lived. I *know.*

But when some crisis puts pressure on my faith; when my peace of mind is blind-sided by some anxiety; when a difficult situation demands that I set aside my own concerns and be thoroughly loving, then I'm like a new driver. I lack the wisdom, the instincts, the reactions. I too often panic and blow it. In the process, I risk my Father's reputation and the welfare of myself and those around me.

Yet I praise the Lord for His patience and His faithful persistence in teaching me. Though I panic, He does not. And I pray that He might help me listen more eagerly, reacting to His teaching as to loving wisdom, and not as if He were trying to meddle in my affairs or limit my freedom. I long for the day when I handle my daily demands as Christ would handle them, exercising His faith and His love.

What does a father do when his son blows it—when he makes a $285 mistake? I explained what he did wrong, then forgave him on the spot—gladly and completely. After all, he was doing his best. I am sympathetic with his struggles. It's not easy, and I want to encourage him. I want him to succeed.

And though he's not yet perfect, he's getting better all the time. I'm really rather proud of him.

Father, Forgive

Prayer Response

When blown by the winds of my weakness
On the sea of my self-centered ways,
The darkness of guilt and despair settles in,
And I long for the light of Your face.

The shame in my soul weighs so heavy,
That I wrestle to win my release;
But Calvary whispers compassion and love
And forgiveness and freedom and peace.

> Father, forgive.
> Open, I come,
> Depending on Your presence
> And thirsting for Your love.
> Father, forgive.
> Trusting, I come.
> Invited by Your mercy,
> I rest in You alone.

Restore to me the joy of Your salvation,
And draw my heart again to Christ above.
I long to live in Your unbroken presence,
To breathe the constant fellowship of love.

Copyright © 1993 by Pilot Point Music. All rights reserved. Administered by Integrated Copyright Group, Inc., P.O. Box 24149, Nashville, TN 37202.

Father, I praise.
Thankful, I come,
Accepting Your forgiveness,
Rejoicing in Your love.
Father, I praise.
Gladly I come
And fix my eyes on Jesus,
To live for You alone.

You are forgiving and good, O Lord, abounding in love to all who call to you (Psalm 86:5).

4

I LOOK TO YOU, LORD, IN DEVOTION AND PRAISE

I consider everything a loss compared to the surpassing greatness of knowing Christ Jesus my Lord, for whose sake I have lost all things. I consider them rubbish, that I may gain Christ and be found in Him.

PHILIPPIANS 3:8-10

LORD, LIFE BECOMES MORE SIMPLE

Hymn

Lord, life becomes more simple
When all I seek is You,
When walking in Your Spirit
Is all that I pursue,
When knowing You are with me
Is all the light I need,
When all my heart is hungry
For You to shape and lead.

Lord, life is filled with beauty
When I am filled with You,
When You, so kind and patient,
Have made me caring, too.
When I am free to love You
And look to You alone,
Then life has found its sunlight,
And hope has found its home.

Lord Jesus, Sun of Heaven,
Its temple and its light,
Life's goal and its beginning,

*This may be read as a devotional prayer, or may be sung to the tune AURELIA, "The Church's One Foundation."

Copyright © 1993 by Ken Bible. All rights reserved. Administered by Integrated Copyright Group, Inc., P.O. Box 24149, Nashville, TN 37202.

This hymn may be photocopied for noncommercial use by churches or groups that have a blanket license from Christian Copyright Licensing Inc. (CCLI), 6130 N.E. 78th Ct., Suite C-11, Portland, OR 97218-2853; 1-800-234-2446. For any other uses, contact Integrated Copyright Group at the address above.

Love's length and depth and height;
Lord, teach my heart to listen
And rest in simple truth,
To know life's sweetest pleasure:
To know and worship You.

—KEN BIBLE

❖

Holiness

Meditation

Now that you have been set free from sin and have become slaves to God, the benefit you reap leads to holiness, and the result is eternal life (Romans 6:22).

*A*T TIMES "holiness" has seemed an unattractive word to me—stiff and puritanical. Even since becoming a Christian, I've often been uncomfortable with it. I've feared that it would put me in a straitjacket, and be binding and restrictive. How could I ever be "holy" and still live freely and naturally? How could I ever relax and just be myself?

At times "holiness" has been a theological word. I've always believed God wants us to live a holy life and has truly made that life available to us. I can't read the New Testament and honestly believe anything else. But in other respects, when I've listened to theological teaching on the subject, then listened objectively to the Bible, I haven't heard them saying quite the same thing. "Holiness" has involved some theological struggles for me.

And at times "holiness" has been a frustrating word. Are any verses in the Bible more intimidating than these?

Just as he who called you is holy, so be holy in all you do; for it is written: "Be holy, because I am holy" (1 Peter 1:15-16).

Anyone who has tried to discipline himself or herself into practicing a consistently holy life has known plenty of frustration.

But "holiness" has changed for me over the years. I no longer feel it is frustrating, nor do I think of it in theological terms. As I've begun to know Christ more personally and enjoy His presence more moment by moment, as a living Friend, I find I don't want to interrupt that relationship. It means too much to me. And as I've experienced the difference He makes in my thoughts and how I live each day, I want to be led by Him and molded by Him 100 percent. I like life better, and I like myself better, when He is shaping me.

In other words, holiness has become a living relationship with Jesus as a personal being. Holiness is the freedom, the wonderful possibility, of being guided and formed completely by Him. Do you know how exciting and satisfying that is after years of struggling with my own weakness?

I don't mean that I've attained perfection. The more I know Him, the more I realize that I fall short. I still fail at times. But when I do, it's because I have not looked to Him and depended on Him in that situation. When I don't look to Him, I grow self-centered, and my thoughts, words, and actions reflect that self-centeredness.

But forgiveness is immediately available. And when I trust Him, something happens. He interacts with me. He responds to me and helps me respond to Him. He changes my feelings and reactions toward Him and toward those around me.

That makes me love Him and trust Him and desire His constant working in me all the more. Our relationship just keeps growing.

Praise be to the God and Father of our Lord Jesus Christ, who has blessed us . . . with every spiritual blessing in Christ (Ephesians 1:3).

Please Yourself, Lord

Prayer Response

My Lord Jesus,
I am amazed at how much life You have breathed
    into my deadness,
How much loving wisdom
    into my selfish ignorance,
How much consistency,
How much holiness,
How much of Yourself You have breathed
    into me.

Loving Lord,
Almighty God,
Merciful Friend,
This is my prayer today:

> Please Yourself in me;
> Wrap Yourself around my thoughts,
>> permeate my feelings,
>> seize my heart,
>> energize all You have made me;
> Fulfill in me
>> all that Your wisdom has planned and
>> all that Your love has dreamed.
> Lord, please Yourself in me today.

The Need Is in Me

Meditation

*"About Jesus of Nazareth," they replied. "He was
a prophet, powerful in word and deed before God
and all the people. The chief priests and our
rulers handed him over to be sentenced to death,
and they crucified him; but we had hoped that
he was the one who was going to redeem Israel"*
(Luke 24:19-21).

I RECENTLY READ Luke 24:13-35, the story of the
two disciples on the road to Emmaus. The time was
Easter Sunday evening, and the two were walking to a
village outside Jerusalem. They had heard initial reports
of the Resurrection but had not yet believed them. As
they traveled, Jesus joined them, but without being rec-
ognized. He drew them into talking about the events
that troubled them so deeply.

I was struck again by the irony of verse 21. Reflect-
ing on Jesus' crucifixion, they said, "but we had hoped
that he was the one who was going to redeem Israel."
They didn't realize what had happened. The very event
that grieved them was their redemption; and the One
they were mourning as dead was the One who stood before them. *They were staring at what they had hoped and
prayed for, but didn't recognize it.*

I wonder how often we stare at God's answers to
our needs but don't recognize them. Like those two disciples, sometimes our understanding is just too shallow

and time-bound. Sometimes we are looking for the easiest way out, for the quickest relief to our pain.

But sometimes we fail to understand God's answers because we fail to understand the need. We don't realize how deep it goes. We usually think the need is a something or a somebody—somebody other than us, of course. These disciples thought the problem was the Romans. Thus when God promised to save them, they assumed He meant political deliverance. But they themselves were the problem. The sin within each of them was the need. God's efforts were focused on them, not on the Romans.

Maybe that's why I don't understand my difficulties at times, and why I'm frustrated when God's deliverance doesn't come the way I think it should. He's working on the problem all right, but the problem usually isn't the other guy or my circumstances. It's me: my willingness to trust God with my concerns; my willingness to love others even when it's difficult.

We are His project. He is concerned about us, not about some circumstance or building or program. He constantly works to redeem us to the very root of our need. He loves us too much to do otherwise. And He often uses our needs and weaknesses to get our attention and call us to himself.

When the pain is most pressing, He is with you. Look in His face and listen for His loving guidance. Hold steady, and He will do His work in you.

Breath of the Father

Prayer Response

Lord, we look up to You, weary of failure,
Bled by our anxious and self-centered lives.
All that we're asking is all that You offer:
All that You are in the Spirit of Christ.

> Breath of the Father,
> Beauty of Jesus,
> Fulness of God ever flowing within,
> Spirit of wisdom,
> Spirit of power,
> Fountain of love and our freedom from sin.

All of our hungers, our hopes and desires,
Meet and are met in the Source of all life.
Teach us the freedom of trusting You fully,
Resting and walking each day in Your light.

> Breath of the Father,
> Beauty of Jesus,
> Fulness of God ever flowing within,
> Come in Your wisdom,
> Come in Your power,
> Come in Your love and bring freedom in Him.

Copyright © 1989 by Pilot Point Music. All rights reserved. Administered by Integrated Copyright Group, Inc., Box 24149, Nashville, TN 37202.

Empty Glory

Meditation

> *Do nothing out of selfish ambition or vain con-*
> *ceit, but in humility consider others better than*
> *yourselves. Each of you should look not only to*
> *your own interests, but also to the interests of*
> *others* (Philippians 2:3-4).

*T*HE ORIGINAL word translated above as "vain con-
ceit" literally means "empty glory." It contrasts with
God's glory, which is the glow of His presence—God
showing himself to us in all of His beauty, power, and
goodness. And the Scriptures clearly teach that we share
in His glory through His Spirit in us.

> *We, who with unveiled faces all reflect the Lord's*
> *glory, are being transformed into his likeness*
> *with ever-increasing glory, which comes from the*
> *Lord, who is the Spirit* (2 Corinthians 3:18).

This is our true glory: Christ living in us, showing
the glow of His presence, His beauty, power, and goodness through us.

But Satan will tempt us to settle for the "empty glory." According to the Greek lexicon, it is "empty" in the
sense of being "without content, without basis, without
truth; without profit; foolish, senseless." That's an accurate description of the self-centered glory we tend to
seek. It's an accurate description of selfish pride.

Pride comes in a variety of styles and colors: you can find one to fit your own personality. My personal choice is humble pride. It is soft-spoken, tastefully adorned in understatement. It does not boast or even posture. It just meditates on self. It dreams about self. Like all forms of pride, the inner vision that drives it is not God or truth, but self-glorification.

Selfish pride is like lust: in the dark privacy of our hearts, it can stimulate and energize. But when it is brought to the light and exposed in public, it is easily seen as a ridiculous lie. What had puffed us up now makes us hide and choke in shame. Its glory is empty glory—without content, without basis in truth, foolish, senseless.

When Satan tempts you to savor this empty glory, see it as the cheap imitation it is. Turn away from it and embrace Your true glory, the presence of God himself with you and in you.

When I turn away from myself and look to God, it's as if someone opens the windows of my mind and heart. Now the sun is shining, and the air is fresh, and other people float into my heart on the breeze. I pray for them and love them, and in the process I love and worship Christ all the more.

Prayer, and especially praise, sheds the light of truth on who we are. It keeps life in perspective. It liberates us from smallness of pride into the wide-open wonder of God's love.

He is with you now and always. Don't let Satan distract you from Him. Discover and enjoy the wonder of His Being.

Pure Light

Prayer Response

The pure light of Your being
Here and now, Holy God,
Wash the worry and the pride
From our eyes,
And leave Your praise.

The pure light of Your mercy
Here and now, Holy God,
Melt the selfishness and sin
From our hearts,
And shine Your life.

> Speak the Word, speak the Word,
> Let the darkness die
> As our faith lifts up the light.
> Let us see, let us see
> With clearer eyes
> Only You,
> Our Lord,
> Only You.

The pure light of Your being
Here and now, Holy God,
Wash the worry and the pride
From our eyes,
And leave Your peace.

Restlessness

Meditation

Earth has nothing I desire besides you (Psalm 73:25).

I WALK INTO my office at home, and I see stacks and stacks of books, shelf after shelf in every direction. When I bought each of them, I convinced myself they were good and reasonable purchases—yes, even necessary. I had a plan for each of them. And many have been put to good use.

But a large number have remained untouched. I enjoyed acquiring them. Buying them provided a few interesting moments that day. And as I look back, I realize that's why I bought them. When I went to that bookstore, there was an inner restlessness, a reaching for something new that might stimulate my life.

Look at your shelves and closets. Be honest. How many of your purchases are driven by an indefinable discontentment? How often do you search for some spark that might make life just a little better, a little more fulfilling?

Purchasing is only one expression of that restlessness. How many of your desires—both the small, daily ones and those that are deep and long-term—are driven by that same searching? We reach for personal achievement or recognition; for personal pleasure, from eating to immorality; perhaps for travel or a new job. The possibilities are as endless as the varied facets of our personalities. I can't discern your motivations, but I see it in myself: a wanting, a searching, an aspiring and dreaming. The desire usually passes unrecognized. I scratch without even realizing it itches.

As I look back, I see that I satisfy old desires only for new ones to take their place. Seldom do I gain any happiness—a bit of comfort occasionally, but not happiness. Such a pattern can stretch into a lifetime of chasing our tails. Our blind attempts at satisfying ourselves only make our lives more complex through addictions and cumbersome habits. We accumulate "conveniences" to repair and worry about, spending ourselves on "treasures" that just sit on the shelf and mock our weakness. All we buy are new dissatisfactions.

I'm not condemning all these things. I'm only sharing a bit of self-understanding that might help you as well. And I'm sharing a discovery: God does not fit this pattern. I am discovering Him as a real Being, an intriguing Person who is continually with me and lives within me. The more I turn to Him, the more He proves himself fulfilling, on both deep and practical levels—beyond what I ever could have imagined. The more I know Him, the more I want to know Him and interact with Him.

I can't tell you how to lose that restlessness, that itch that expresses itself in so many ways. But you can do what I'm doing: every time you recognize that restlessness, turn it on God. Look to Him instead of to anything else. The more you carry your needs and desires to Him, the more you'll discover that *He* is your joy. *He* is that stimulation and inner spark. And He will be as satisfying and personal to you as you let Him be.

Loving Christ—truly loving *Him*—can simplify life.

Psalm of Trust

Prayer Response

As the thirsty long for water
In a dry and lonely place,
So, my Lord, I long to know You,
Long to simply see Your face.
Lord, just now, as I am looking,
Let me simply see Your face.

As a servant to his master,
So to You I lift my eyes—
You, my God, so high and holy;
"Mercy, Lord!" is all I cry.
In this need and utter weakness
"Mercy, Lord!" is all I cry.

As a baby with its mother,
Quiet, nestled on her breast,
I'm Your child—I know You love me;
Lord, I lean on You and rest.
Quiet, now I quit my struggling;
Lord, I lean on You and rest.

As Your lamb, You daily guide me
Into pastures rich with food.
Lord, no matter where You lead me,
I am always here with You!
By the waters, through the valleys
I will always be with You!

Based on Psalms 42, 123, 131, and 23

One Thing I Seek

Meditation

Whom have I in heaven but you? . . . My flesh and my heart may fail, but God is the strength of my heart and my portion forever (Psalm 73:25-26).

*W*HEN I CAN finally see God for all that He is to me—
all that He always has been and always will be—
so that anxiety and fear are lost in total trust;
When I have truly grasped His love,
so that joy and rest and belonging
are deep and rich and constant;
When I am filled and dominated and totally led by His
Spirit
so that every desire, every thought,
every motion of my being
is in Him and prompted by Him;
What hunger will be left?

Psalm 27 expresses it this way:
One thing I ask of the LORD, this is what I seek: that I may dwell in the house of the LORD all the days of my life, to gaze upon the beauty of the LORD and to seek him (v. 4).

When I see Him fully and trust Him completely, the only thing I will still hunger for is *Him*. All the beauty and glory and abundance of heaven will come from one Source: God himself. We will never be anything but completely dependent on Him—not on His gifts, but on Him.

Revelation 21:22-23 says that in His immediate presence, we will need no temple, sun, or moon. He himself is our warmth, our light, and our worship.

In His personal presence, Jesus' simple statements about himself become personal truth:

> I am the bread of life. He who comes to me will never go hungry, and he who believes in me will never be thirsty (John 6:35).

> I am the light of the world. Whoever follows me will never walk in darkness (John 8:12).

> I am the resurrection and the life. . . . Whoever lives and believes in me will never die (John 11:25-26).

> I am the Alpha and the Omega, the Beginning and the End. To him who is thirsty I will give to drink without cost from the spring of the water of life (Revelation 21:6).

Your heart can be captured by the living beauty—and simplicity—of the personal Christ. That beauty holds a bonding that grows stronger and stronger, prayer by prayer. As we trust Him and love Him, we find our needs and hungers met in Him. Every lesser desire gradually disappears into Him. And in knowing and interacting with such a wonderful, infinite God, we never get to the point of feeling, "OK, that's enough." Even in our joyful satisfaction, the hunger remains, continuing to draw us into a fuller friendship with Him.

All of history, all the vast universe—seen and unseen—and all the desires and hopes of humanity are summed up in Christ (Ephesians 1:9-10). That summing up is also an individual process. Let Him start it in you now. Let Him begin it in your heart, and He will spread it throughout your thoughts and feelings, your attitudes and your life-style.

He has not put eternity's best blessings out of your reach. They are as near as His presence, as near as looking to Him in simple faith.

❖

More

Prayer Response

Jesus,
I am finding You
More than a promise,
More than a hope,
More than a shadow in my mind.

You are
More than I have let You be,
More than I can imagine You to be,
More than all the dreams
    that have cluttered my mind;

You are all the "more" of my restless desires,
All the "more" of God's restless love for me,
All the "more" of eternity
    Ever here, ever flowing,

Ever full, yet ever growing,
Ever satisfying and
Ever surprising.

Jesus,
To You be all my love and trust,
    all my hungering and hoping,
    all my living and rejoicing and aspiring,
Look by look, Lord,
More and more.

Creation's Prayer

Meditation

All you have made will praise you, O LORD
(Psalm 145:10).

ON A SATURDAY morning in spring I was trekking through woods near my home. At one point, a dead tree caught my eye. It was taller than the green trees around it, and its branches were high, close to the trunk, and pointing upward. Against the clear blue sky, the tree seemed to stand in solemn silence, lifting praise to God in an endless liturgy.

That one glimpse helped me see again that all creation is God's temple, quietly but constantly reminding us that

He is *here;*

He is *great,* beyond our imaginations;

He is *love:* He lavishes himself upon us, holding nothing back.

When I look at creation and believe that He shaped it all for His purposes, I realize I am surrounded by many liturgies to God. Each tells us about Him in ways that are more universal, more lasting, and more tangible than human language. I look into the night sky and am awestruck by His vastness. I swing through the round of day and night, season after season, and experience His unchanging faithfulness. The incredible network of life that packs every layer of our world, from water drops to endless oceans, paints Him as a fountain of rich, un-bounded life. And every breath I take reminds me that He shares His eternal life with me.

I live in a natural world that stands in a constant attitude of prayer to God. Its attitude is dependence:

All look to you to give them their food at the proper time. . . . When you open your hand, they are satisfied with good things (Psalm 104:27-28).

Its attitude is praise:

The heavens declare the glory of God; the skies proclaim the work of his hands. Day after day they pour forth speech; night after night they display knowledge. There is no speech or language where their voice is not heard. Their voice goes out into all the earth, their words to the ends of the world (Psalm 19:1-4).

Creation reminds me that the truest trust, the most profound prayer, the deepest worship we offer God is not expressed in words. Such prayer is expressed in being and doing. It is not heard in church services or read in books. It is seen in the faithful lives of His people, living to God and for God and in God, day after day, age after age.

I want to be part of that prayer. I want my whole life to sing trust and praise and love to Him, faithfully and constantly, forever and ever.

Creation Praise

Prayer Response

I open my eyes
And finally see
What always has been.
I breathe the beauty of Your presence
In the morning air.

Lord, here in Your temple,
With mountains and meadows
In holy array,
I hear Your liturgy arising
In unceasing praise.

> Even dead trees dance,
> And the silent sing,
> And the night sky glows
> With the love of our Father.
> My Creator Lord,
> Give my heart a voice.
> Let me join in praise
> To Your glory, O God—
> To Your glory, O God.

Your wisdom and love,
Compassion and power
Take color and form,
With days and seasons ever singing
Of Your faithful care.

Lord, all that I am
Is born of Your Being
And springs from Your heart.
We're rising from and through and to You
In unending life.

    Even dead trees dance,
    And the silent sing,
    And the night sky glows
    With the love of our Father.
    My Creator Lord,
    Give my heart a voice.
    Let me join in praise
    To Your glory, O God;
    To Your glory, O God.

5

I LOOK TO YOU, LORD, IN MY RELATIONSHIPS

God is love. Whoever lives in love lives in God, and God in him.

1 JOHN 4:16

I LOOK TO YOU, AND YOU ARE LOVE

Hymn

I look to You, and You are love,
And Father, You are here.
While close to You, my heart is love,
And praise replaces fear.

> *Refrain:*
> *My Lord, my God, You're with me now;*
> *I love, and I am free.*
> *Stay near and breathe just one desire:*
> *To love as You love me.*

I pray, and Lord, I see Your face
In family and friends.
The love that binds my heart to You
Now binds my heart to them.

> *Refrain:*
> *My Lord, my God, You're with me now;*
> *I love, and I am free.*
> *Stay near and breathe just one desire:*
> *To love as You love me.*

*This may be read as a devotional prayer, or may be sung to the tune LANDAS, "My Faith Has Found a Resting Place."

Copyright © 1993 by Ken Bible. All rights reserved. Administered by Integrated Copyright Group, Inc., P.O. Box 24149, Nashville, TN 37202.

This hymn may be photocopied for noncommercial use by churches or groups that have a blanket license from Christian Copyright Licensing, Inc. (CCLI), 6130 N.E. 78th Ct., Suite C-11, Portland, OR 97218-2853; 1-800-234-2446. For any other uses, contact Integrated Copyright Group at the address above.

I face You, Lord, and know Your love
And know it has no bounds.
I long to bring that love to life
And spread it all around.

> *Refrain:*
> *My Lord, my God, You're with me now;*
> *I love, and I am free.*
> *Stay near and breathe just one desire:*
> *To love as You love me.*

—KEN BIBLE

Knowledge, Prophecy, and Love

Meditation

Knowledge puffs up, but love builds up (1 Corinthians 8:1).

*I*MAGINE how our society would rank the following in relative value:

a highly intelligent person
one who could foretell the future
a very loving person

Which would command respect, attention, and a large salary? It's a rhetorical question. Intelligent people are put on a pedestal. Prophets are almost gods. And being loving—well, it's "nice" and perhaps admirable, but not highly esteemed nor ambitiously sought.

But as I read 1 Corinthians 13, I'm struck by how strongly it emphasizes the opposite mind-set. Of 13 verses, 6 cover the relative worthlessness of knowledge and prophecy as compared to love.

Love never fails. But where there are prophecies, they will cease; where there are tongues, they will be stilled; where there is knowledge, it will pass away. For we know in part and we prophesy in part, but when perfection comes, the imperfect disappears. When I was a child, I talked like a child, I thought like a child, I reasoned like a child. When I became a man, I put childish ways behind me. Now we see but a poor reflection as in a mirror; then we shall see face to face. Now I know in part; then I shall know fully, even as I am fully known. And now these three remain: faith, hope and love. But the greatest of these is love (vv. 8-13).

Paul's point is that knowledge and prophecy are quickly obsolete. They are always so partial and temporary. We think of knowledge as the golden apple, the elusive key to life, but time washes it down its sewer along with everything else of passing value. Knowledge quickly becomes stale. Is anything more riddled with error than an old science text? The scientific theories of each age seem to have one thing in common: they are eventually shown to be highly inadequate or downright inaccurate.

True prophecies are rare, but even they, once fulfilled, simply become part of yesterday's newspaper.

Love is the one treasure that time and change will never supercede. It becomes more precious as the years pass.

And if You want an idea of what eternity will be like, don't just turn to knowledge and prophecy—think of love. Think of the time when you sensed the most deeply that God loved you. Remember the many ways He has surrounded you with His love and has slipped unexpected blessings into Your life. And consider how wonderful, fulfilling, and mysterious love can be between two people.

Now, imagine that love perfected and fully realized, saturating every aspect of your thinking and feeling. We will all interact openly and naturally, unimpaired by any selfishness or weakness. Imagine such a relationship with every other being. Imagine such a relationship with God.

Love, even in its simplest expressions, is an eternal treasure. It is worth including among our life ambitions. Love is worth consulting and following in each daily decision. It is the quality that best helps us understand God's heart.

Perhaps the sweetest reward of standing in God's presence is being able to experience His love more personally. As we speak with Him more constantly and more openly, His presence and His love grow more real. We begin to know the joy of returning that love, and of having it flavor our relationships with those around us.

The greatest of these is love. Pursue love (1 Corinthians 13:13-14:1, NASB).

Nurture Our Love

Prayer Response

Lord,
As I know You,
I know love.
Nurture my knowing.
Nurture our love.
Let it grow as broad
    and as giving in me
As it is in You.

Preoccupied with Love

Meditation

Do everything in love (1 Corinthians 16:14).

*W*HEN YOUR mind wanders, where does it go? What do you think about in your spare moments—while driving, eating, waiting, or doing undemanding tasks? What are your daydreams?

During a recent vacation, I was in the same room with a number of family members, all near and dear to me. Yet I caught myself being so self-absorbed that my heart and mind were not awake to them and their concerns. If they had felt problems or pain or confusion, I wouldn't have sensed it. I wouldn't have reached out to them to offer a listening heart.

The Lord has graciously showed me that I waste too much of my time and thought on myself.

I want to be preoccupied with loving other people. What could I accomplish if I let the Lord's love dream through me?

I want to be awake to the kaleidoscope of concerns around me, ready to be Christ's presence however I can.

I want to be more Christlike. I'm tired of being insensitive in the little things I say and in the little things I don't say. I want to have the mind and heart of Christ.

How does this happen, after a lifetime of being self-centered? Resolutions and guilt trips don't work. But I'm finding the answer is much simpler. Whenever I realize that I stand in Christ's presence, my heart is drawn to Him in prayer. And as I turn to Him, He soon brings other people to mind. When I pray, He frees me from bondage to myself and into the freedom of love. And I can pray anytime.

Sitting in church on a Sunday morning, I find myself praying for the needs around me:

> to my right, a family numb from years of dealing with a delinquent son;

> behind me, the husband apparently about to lose his elderly wife;

> off to my left, the head of the local rescue mission, here on his one day off from his draining duties;

> in front, the mother of two young children, facing a painful divorce.

In traffic, passing coworkers in the office, or in my home, He is ready to share His mind and heart with me. He just calls me to turn to Him more often as I live in His presence.

Lord, draw me to You.

This Moment

Prayer Response

Right now, Father,
What should my concerns be?
Let Your love lead me this moment.

When the "Me" Becomes "We"

Meditation

All the believers were one in heart and mind. No one claimed that any of his possessions was his own, but they shared everything they had. . . . There were no needy persons among them (Acts 4:32, 34).

*D*REAM with me for a moment.

First, think of how much time and energy you spend on your personal needs and concerns. Consider how many of your thoughts are lavished on making yourself look good in others' eyes and on fulfilling your own dreams.

Now think of being made one with Christ. Second Corinthians 3:18 says that as the Holy Spirit helps us look to Christ, we are being made more like Him. And in 1 John 3:2 we're told:

When he appears, we shall be like him, for we shall see him as he is.

Realize that when each of us is made completely like Christ, we become one with each other as well. We will be one in Him. Not only will I, individually, be all God's love has planned for me, but we, corporately, will be as well. All the little, passing things that divide us will be washed away—all the insecurities, the remains of foolish selfishness, the physical, cultural, and emotional barriers, our inability to see ourselves and each other accurately. We will all be one, naturally and completely—one with a glorified creation; one with each other; one with the Father, Son, and Spirit.

Unity and individuality will be brought to full bloom together. Love will be open, comfortable, and complete, the motivator for every thought and action. Peace and wholeness will be a reality.

Imagine what life will be like when the energies we invest in "me" are focused entirely on the "we." And that "we" will be all of us together with Christ himself. Imagine how that will affect:

our work

our fellowship together

our worship

Imagine the freedom when all hindrances to full, heartfelt praise are gone. We will see Christ as He is and live in His immediate presence, fully responding to all He is. All we see and sense around us will be filled with His life and His holiness. All will sing with one heart:

Holy, holy, holy is the LORD Almighty; the whole earth is full of his glory (Isaiah 6:3).

What will our worship, love, and fellowship be then?

But these blessings are not entirely part of the future. Even now each believer shares the same Spirit, the same mind and heart of Christ.

There is one body and one Spirit . . . one Lord, one faith . . . one God and Father of all, who is over all and through all and in all (Ephesians 4:4-5).

To the degree that we listen to His Spirit and walk in His Spirit, moment by moment, we *are* one with

Christ and one with each other. Imagine how wonderful our unity would be now if we would:

> *Be completely humble and gentle; be patient, bearing with one another in love. Make every effort to keep the unity of the Spirit through the bond of peace* (Ephesians 4:2-3).

> *Each of you should look not only to your own interests, but also to the interests of others* (Philippians 2:4).

> *Above all, love each other deeply* (1 Peter 4:8).

Love and unity are wonderful blessings, not just someday, but today. He calls us to treasure them and nurture them now.

But He doesn't ask us to do it in our own power. His Spirit breathes in us naturally as we open ourselves to Him in a life of prayer.

Speaking and Listening

Prayer Response

Father, I need Your Spirit living in me constantly.
We need Your Spirit in each of us, and among us.
But we hear Your warning:

> *Do not grieve the Holy Spirit of God* (Ephesians 4:30).

Do not cause Him sorrow or pain.

Do not destroy the joy He has planted in you.
And:

> *Do not put out the Spirit's fire* (1 Thessalonians 5:19).

Do not hinder His working among you.
Do not ignore His wisdom or frustrate His love.

Lord, how do I grieve You?
What do I do that causes You pain?

> *Therefore each of you must put off falsehood and speak truthfully to his neighbor, for we are all members of one body. . . . Do not let any unwholesome talk come out of your mouths, but only what is helpful for building others up according to their needs, that it may benefit those who listen. And do not grieve the Holy Spirit of God . . . Get rid of all bitterness, rage and anger, brawling and slander, along with every form of malice* (Ephesians 4:25, 29-31).

I grieve You by what I say to my fellow believers.
I wound You with words spoken against
> my brothers and sisters,
> words that are careless, angry, hasty, self-serving.

When I hurt any member of Your Body, You feel the pain.

And how do I quench Your Spirit?
What do I do that hinders Your work?

> *Do not put out the Spirit's fire; do not treat prophecies with contempt. Test everything. Hold on to the good. Avoid every kind of evil* (1 Thessalonians 5:19-22).

When I fail to listen when other believers speak,
When I turn them off without hearing them,
I am ignoring You.

For Your words don't usually come to us
　　through a booming voice from heaven,
And prophecies are not just predictions of the future,
　　thundered by strange men dressed in camel's hair.
But through ordinary human lips Your Spirit speaks
　　Your guidance, warning, comfort, and love.
Your precious wisdom is delivered by
Your children.

Savior, help me cherish Your presence
　　in each of my brothers and sisters.
As I speak to them,
　　may I always do so with the love I owe You.
As they speak to me,
　　let me listen from my heart and hear
　　Your voice,
　　my loving Lord.

Praying for Fellow Workers

Meditation

Submit to one another out of reverence for Christ (Ephesians 5:21).

I urge, then, first of all, that requests, prayers, intercession and thanksgiving be made for everyone—for . . . all those in authority (1 Timothy 2:1-2).

*W*E ALL HAVE to work with other people, whether on our jobs, at home, or in the church. And often, our work is interconnected. If someone else doesn't do a good job, the quality and success of our own work is affected.

We also work with people in authority over us. We are forced to depend on their wisdom and understanding to make the right decisions.

Both of these groups are largely beyond our control, and yet they seriously affect our work. Dealing with that fact, with that limitation, can be very frustrating.

When I write a song lyric, I depend on the composer. My work will fly or fail, depending on his or her musical setting. When I'm responsible for a recording project, so much relies on the producer. If his or her work is careful and creative, the recording will sparkle. If not, nothing can make it succeed. And yes, I have managers over me, and their decisions on key questions define my job.

In recent years, my responsibilities have left me increasingly dependent on such fellow workers. In dealing with a number of stressful situations, the Lord has brought me back to the above verses, about submitting to one another and praying for one another. I'm discovering that is great, practical advice.

Instead of fretting about whether another person will do his or her job well, or whether a supervisor will make the right decision, I'm learning to pray for them. I pray that God will guide them and work through them to accomplish His perfect will.

Then, having prayed for them and trusted the Lord to work through them, I can more easily rely on them and be submissive to them. And when I still feel I must disagree, I can do so in a nondefensive, nonterritorial manner, remembering it is God's work, not mine, and He will accomplish it.

Sometimes we assume that if everyone would just leave us alone, if we weren't so dependent on others, everything would be terrific. But the Bible declares that that simply isn't so. Each of us has a particular role to play. By ourselves, we have severe limitations. We were designed to work most efficiently and productively in relationship to others. We are each like one part of the body that must work with other parts if the whole body is to function successfully. God created us to be dependent not only on himself but on each other.

Prayer is the best way to make that relationship work. Through prayer, we lift up those on whom we are dependent. Through prayer, we maintain the right attitude toward them. Prayer for our fellow workers fosters the unity and interdependence essential for all of us to be and do our best together.

And through prayer, we keep our faith focused on God's will and on His ability to accomplish that will through us, not just through me.

I Bring That One to You

Prayer Response

Lord, I bring that one to You.
Bless this person with Your wisdom,
    Your presence,
    Your very best;
And keep me humble, our Father,
    before them
    and before You.

Musical and Spiritual Changes

Meditation

We have not stopped praying for you and asking God to fill you with the knowledge of his will . . . We pray this in order that you may live a life worthy of the Lord and may please him in every way (Colossians 1:9-10).

ONE OF MY recent assignments was to direct the compilation of a new hymnal. I was amazed again at how strongly and emotionally people feel about their own musical tastes. Some truly important issues can be greeted with deafening indifference—but not music.

That is especially true with teenagers. With three in our house, I can affirm what you already know: they have their own ideas about music. Yes, we can expose them to various styles and set limits on their listening. But their musical tastes are part of their independence as people. Their music is THEIRS, and they are absolutely fierce in clinging to it. Hands off!

But it's been fascinating to watch my eldest son, Jason. A few years ago he would only listen to the loudest, most aggressive contemporary music. He scorned anything else. But by his later years in high school, his musical tastes had mellowed and matured. The music he now buys is still contemporary, but it also has clear echoes of folk and traditional elements in it. It's less abrasive and more subtle and creative. My wife and I actually enjoy much of it.

How did these changes happen? As a gradual process, I imagine. As he grew and changed and was exposed to more music, old styles wore thin and became juvenile. His friends certainly played a major part. They shared their sounds, and their enthusiasm. Over time, he acquired a taste for those sounds and embraced them as his own.

These musical changes have brought me hope that other changes will happen with my children—internal changes. My greatest hope and prayer is that someday they will embrace Christ and the Christian life with the enthusiasm they show toward their music—that it is THEIRS, and no one can take it away.

How might this happen? Time, maturity, and the Christian influence of friends will probably play a part. I'm also sure our influence will be strong in their lives. Though our children seem to turn off much of what we *tell* them, I know they watch us. When I was young and uncertain about what to expect from the future, I watched my elders closely and learned all I could from their lives. Our children are doing the same thing. How vital it is, then, that we live daily as in God's presence:

> *Live a life worthy of the calling you have re-*
> *ceived. . . . Live a life of love . . . You were once*
> *darkness, but now you are light in the Lord. Live*
> *as children of light* (Ephesians 4:1; 5:2, 8).

But I am also encouraged as I remember that the same God who has been at work in me all these years is also at work in them. The Holy Spirit operates patiently but so powerfully. He is not some weak and wispy "spirit" with limited ability to touch and move and make changes. He is as strong and zealous and ardently loving as Almighty God himself. And He works effectively where it matters most: in the hearts and minds of individuals.

As I turn to God and pray for my teens as they enter my mind, I do so with the confidence that day by day, circumstance by circumstance, God is lovingly and faithfully pursuing their deepest affections.

❖

Our Father

Prayer Response

My Father and
The Father of my children,
Make me a spring of Your love in
 their lives.
May they know the fragrance
 of Your presence
 through me.

Individuals, Not Issues

Meditation

If you really keep the royal law found in Scripture, "Love your neighbor as yourself," you are doing right (James 2:8).

I REMEMBER when my brother first told us he was gay. For a while, homosexuality itself was the issue. He was anxious for us to understand him and be open to his viewpoint. We were somewhat anxious to let him know we didn't read the Bible that way.

But eventually, we moved beyond dealing with homosexuality as an issue and got down to personal relationships. The real question for me became:

How do I treat my brother who is gay?

The answer soon became obvious: I love him like my brother. That's my sole responsibility toward him. It's really that simple.

Then the broader question for me, and for all of us, is:

How do we treat our "neighbors" who are gay?

And again the answer is simple and obvious: we love them like neighbors. We love them as we love ourselves.

The natural concern may be, "But aren't we obligated to let them know we don't condone their life-style?" Believe me, gays are deeply and painfully aware that society doesn't approve of them. They don't need reminders.

The real question for us is: have we shown them that Christ likes them and loves them, personally and unconditionally?

When Jesus was on earth, He was accused of being a friend to those considered morally repulsive. "Religious" people wouldn't get near them, but He hung around them, went to their parties, and in general, seemed to like them and care about them. And they liked Him and listened to Him.

While we tend to focus on issues and overlook individuals, Christ did the opposite. He looked past politics and concentrated on persons.

In that spirit, my point is not political or social, but personal. Our responsibility is not to try to change people. We are not responsible to try to convert homosexuals into heterosexuals. Our challenge is first and foremost to be Christlike so that people are attracted to Him. And we can't do that as long as we're fearfully shaking our fingers in their faces.

Nothing should ever distract us from showing that genuine, face-to-face love of Christ. Nothing. He is the force who changes hearts, not laws.

Do I pray for my brother? Of course. Frequently. I pray for him just as I pray for all those I love: that he would experience the full pleasure of serving Christ and living each day with Him and in Him.

Responding as to You

Prayer Response

In every relationship
Help me react in Your Spirit, with
    Your gentleness and
    Your compassion,
Responding not as to an adversary,
But as to You,
    My loving Savior.

6

I LOOK TO YOU, LORD, IN MY SERVICE TO YOU

"Not by might nor by power, but by my Spirit,"
says the LORD *Almighty.*

ZECHARIAH 4:6

FRUITFUL IN YOU

Hymn

Only in You, my Lord,
Only in You;
Simply available
For You to use;
Letting You lead, I prove
Fruitful, my Lord, in You;
Fruitful in You,
Fruitful in You.

Only for You, my Lord,
Only for You;
Each act an offering
For You to use;
Living in love, I prove
Fruitful, my Lord, in You;
Fruitful in You,
Fruitful in You.

Only through prayer, my Lord,
Only through prayer;
Simply and constantly,
Knowing You're there;

*This may be read as a devotional prayer, or may be sung to the tune MORE LOVE TO THEE.

Copyright © 1993 by Ken Bible. All rights reserved. Administered by Integrated Copyright Group, Inc., P.O. Box 24149, Nashville, TN 37202.

This hymn may be photocopied for noncommercial use by churches or groups that have a blanket license from Christian Copyright Licensing Inc. (CCLI), 6130 N.E. 78th Ct., Suite C-11, Portland, OR 97218-2853; 1-800-234-2446. For any other uses, contact Integrated Copyright Group at the address above.

Sharing Your life, I prove
Fruitful, my Lord, in You;
Fruitful in You,
Fruitful in You.

—Ken Bible

❖

Only by the Lord

Meditation

I am the vine; you are the branches. If a man re-mains in me and I in him, he will bear much fruit; apart from me you can do nothing (John 15:5).

*M*Y FRUITFULNESS flows from the presence of Christ within me. I am completely dependent on His working in and through me.

That's why my devotional life is so critical—not just in those special private times but also as I look to Him throughout the day. Such prayer keeps me in touch with Him and open to His influence. Without it, I tend to sink into preoccupation with myself and lesser concerns.

Being a writer teaches me this dependence more than anything else ever has. Every morning when I get up to write, I have to face my own inability and release the work to Him:

"Lord, this time is Yours.

I can only work as You enable me.

I look to You now and will just follow as You lead."

This is especially necessary when the task gets difficult. When I get stuck at a specific spot, my first instinct is to press harder. I want to get past the frustration and finish the job. But I'm learning I have to stop and pray,

"Lord, I did not choose my task,

nor can I make it happen.

But my Father,

I am simply available to You."

I have to open myself to Him and wait, letting Him work in His way and time. And He does—beautifully, bringing me solutions and directions I never could have found on my own.

Frequently the wait is relatively short. Something unexplainable just happens when I release the task to Him. He works so naturally and perfectly.

Yet sometimes the wait is longer. I'm forced to live with unfinished business, and I can become anxious and discouraged. During such times, I repeatedly go to Him, intent on talking about the "doing." But He wants to talk about "us." He reminds me to look at Him, enjoy. Him, and be at peace in Him. He invites me to just rest in His "doing."

I am the vine; you are the branches. If a man remains in me and I in him, he will bear much fruit; apart from me you can do nothing (John 15:5).

"Remain in him" by turning to Him throughout the day. It will help keep your heart set on Him. And you will know that He, himself, is life's sweetest gift and the source of all of our fruitfulness.

The Tree of Prayer

Prayer Response

Lord,
I love You,
And I need You.
Let the tree of prayer grow
	taller and stronger in me.

Only for the Lord

Meditation

If we live, we live to the Lord, and if we die, we die to the Lord; so then, whether we live or whether we die, we are the Lord's (Romans 14:8, NRSV).

THOUGH I HAVE never been a pastor, I know I am called to full-time Christian service. God has led and prepared and commissioned me. He has given me a burning desire to communicate His truth in a way that is fresh and penetrating, yet practical.

As a result, I have spent my entire adult life employed by Christian organizations. I consider that a great privilege and joy.

But that doesn't mean all has been sweetness and light. My bosses have been as human as any other bosses. My jobs have often been filled with stress, frustration, and unending setbacks. Often I have felt my employers were not worthy of the dedication I was giving. I felt unappreciated. And many times I have feared that when all is said and done, my efforts would be meaningless.

Because of all this, I have reminded myself of the following over and over again throughout my working life:

I do not work for my bosses.

I do not work for the company.

I don't even work for the Church.

I work for the Lord.

Do my bosses seem unfair and misguided? I do not work for them. I work for the Lord.

Does my pay seem far less than what I deserve? I work for the Lord. He provides abundantly for me, and I owe Him everything.

Does my work seem trivial and meaningless? I do it because He has called me, and He feels it is important. My work is a personal "Thank You!" to Him, trusting He will bless it as a seed and make it grow.

During my frustrations I can lift myself and my job to Him. I can release them to Him knowing He has put me here. It is His work, and He is here with me. Such prayer helps me look in a different direction. It turns my heart away from my selfish interests and toward His purpose and glory.

Doing the work then becomes a prayer in itself, a way of acting out my trust and love for Him.

No matter what your present job, use it to serve your Lord joyfully. Bring your work to Him, and do it for Him. He is a wonderful employer!

Slaves, obey your earthly masters in everything; and do it, not only when their eye is on you and to win their favor, but with sincerity of heart and reverence for the Lord. Whatever you do, work at it with all your heart, as working for the Lord, not for men (Colossians 3:22-23).

I Work for You

Prayer Response

As long as I am on this job, Lord,
    I will do it for You.
When I quit,
    It will be for Your reasons, not mine.
Until then, I will do what pleases You:
    I will persevere;
    I will be faithful;
    I will live only to glorify You.

Thank You, Lord, for Your daily strength.

Breakfast with the Lord

Meditation

Do you truly love me more than these? (John 21:15).

*P*LEASE TAKE a few minutes to read John 21:1-22.

This is such a simple, natural scene—real people in a relaxed setting. There is daily, common labor. The work seems frustrating, but when the Lord blesses it, it is abundantly rewarding.

Jesus is there on the shore, resurrected and very real. But we see no flashes of light, no walking through walls. He's just squatting on the ground, quietly cooking breakfast over an open fire. It's an unpretentious meal, eaten with close, comfortable friends.

Jesus is present, face to face.

He blesses their work.

He provides for their daily needs and shares these average moments with them.

That's where I need Jesus in my life: across the breakfast table; on my job; helping me through the long nights of frustration; providing for the needs that keep coming day by day. In the routine, His presence is the most real and meaningful to me.

But it's also where I hear His probing question:

Do you truly love me more than these?

And I hear echoes of His command and promise:
*Seek first his kingdom and his righteousness,
and all these things [food, clothing, life's necessi-
ties] will be given to you as well* (Matthew 6:33).

I get so preoccupied with my own concerns. I think
that if this one need were met, I would enjoy the
essence of well-being. But Jesus calls me to seek Him
first, His kingdom and His righteousness, resting all my
needs with the Father.

I long for each of my relationships to be everything
I dream it should be. He calls me to simply love everyone around me, unselfishly, with practical kindness.

On the job, my concern is to achieve that one de-
sired area of service. He calls me to glorify Him no matter where He puts me. He asks that I feed His sheep in
whatever assignment I face.

There He is, across the table. He hands me my daily provisions. I face Him as I face my day. Can I tell
Him I love Him more than anything else, right here and
now? That is what His eyes ask. That is what He seeks
of me.

And as I spend time with Him, how can I help but
say,

Yes, Lord . . . I love you (John 21:15).

Closer, Lord

Prayer Response

I have responsibilities.
I have needs and concerns.

But Lord, let me dwell on them
    only as much as
Faith permits and
Love demands.

Instead of allowing them to
Distract me from You,
Let's share them, Lord.
Through them, draw me closer to You,
    Beautiful God.
Let them become opportunities to
    Love You and
    Trust You and
    Make You real to those around me.

Spirit of Christ,
Breathe my every thought.
Fill my mind,
    My imagination,
    My dreams
With Your love and
The wonder of Your presence.

You are my Lord forever!

What Does Your Faith Demand?

Meditation

I do not have time to tell about Gideon, Barak, Samson, Jephthah, David, Samuel and the prophets, who through faith conquered kingdoms, administered justice, and gained what was promised; who shut the mouths of lions, quenched the fury of the flames, and escaped the edge of the sword; whose weakness was turned to strength. . . . These were all commended for their faith (Hebrews 11:32-34, 39).

DO YOU realize the faith you cherish in your heart has changed all of reality for you? Past, present, and future are all different because you trust Christ.

The past is different because all your sins are gone. God does not remember them against you any more.

The present is different because He is with you and within you always. You please your holy Father by simply trusting Him.

The future is different because you have an unshakable, unchangeable hope. The God who revealed himself to you will one day reveal himself fully, and you will live in His presence forever.

That is a powerful and valuable faith. And it is the very same faith that lived in Peter and the apostle Paul,

Augustine and John Calvin, Martin Luther and John Wesley. The very same faith.

I look at what those people accomplished in their days—actually, what God accomplished through them. It becomes apparent that they lived as they did because of what they believed.

The apostle Paul believed in the gospel of Christ. He had met the resurrected Christ and had experienced transformation. So when he was called to share that gospel with those who hadn't heard, he did so energetically, traveling, writing, and enduring more than most people would in 10 lifetimes.

Martin Luther believed in salvation by faith alone. So when he was called before the religious leaders of his day, under tremendous pressure to recant, he answered, "Here I stand . . . I can do no other." Church history was changed forever.

John Wesley believed that God provides holy hearts and holy lives, so he lived it and taught it and encouraged it. He believed that God wanted the average man on the street to hear the gospel, so he preached it in the open air, though the church of his day considered that scandalous. And he believed that God still cared about prostitutes, orphans, prisoners, and drunkards, so he aggressively ministered to them in practical ways.

If these Christian brothers were to stand before us now, I'm sure they would say these accomplishments weren't the result of superhuman heroism or some ability of their own. They simply trusted God one step at a time, and did what their faith demanded of them, even when it flew in the face of all that was "accepted" in their day.

What do you believe?

What do your beliefs demand of you?

You are standing in Jesus' presence now, surrounded by needy persons whom He longs to love. Turn to Him and listen. What is He asking You to do? Don't be overwhelmed by the size of the need. Just do the one thing He gives you to do, then keep listening and obeying. Leave the need in His hands.

❖

I Cannot Live Half-heartedly

Prayer Response

Father, You love with a burning love.
I cannot stand before You
And live half-heartedly.
Speak, Lord, and
I will listen.
I will trust.
I will follow You.

Ask Anything in My Name

Meditation

I tell you the truth, my Father will give you whatever you ask in my name. Until now you have not asked for anything in my name. Ask and you will receive, and your joy will be complete (John 16:23-24).

DURING JESUS' final session with His disciples before His crucifixion (John 13—17), He talked to them about their ministry after His departure. Four different times (John 14:13-14; 15:7; 15:16; 16:23-24) He said,

Then the Father will give you whatever you ask in my name (John 15:16).

These verses are intriguing because they sound like a blank check. Rub the lamp and make three wishes. But we seem to assume that either our faith isn't strong enough, or that the "fine print" makes these verses of little practical significance to us. In any case, we don't take Jesus' offer very seriously.

Recently, however, I looked into the contexts to understand what He was so anxious to tell us.

—He emphasized that we were to ask in His name; that is, within His will, and only for His purposes (14:13; 15:16; 16:23-24).

—He repeatedly said the reason our prayers would be answered is that the Father might be glorified (14:13; 15:8), and that we might bear fruit to Him (15:16).

—Jesus makes it clear that we will share His own direct relationship with the Father (16:23-24, 26-27). As we live in His Spirit, depending on the Father, willing only what He wills, we can ask boldly and largely on behalf of His work.

In this light, these "ask anything" verses are not an option or an invitation to self-indulgence. They are a challenge to ministry.

Think of the ministry God has given you. Are your desires focused enough on Him that You truly want only what He wants, and only for His glory? If so, is your faith aggressive enough to believe He can do more than you can do on your own? Do you limit your service to levels in which you can operate comfortably on your own strength? Or do you let Him lead you into tasks where you have to depend on Him?

"Ask anything in my name" is a call to walk in His Spirit, meeting each challenge with simple, assured prayer.

Does Christ repeatedly point you to any area of service or obedience? Perhaps you've tried to avoid it as being unrealistic or beyond you. But He gently, persistently brings it back to your mind. Face it with Him, step by step, prayer by prayer. You'll be surprised at how He can work through you.

Breathe Every Prayer

Prayer Response

My mind is Yours.
My voice is Yours.
Each moment is Yours.
Breathe every prayer, Lord.
Be the Servant Christ
In me today.

Serving in Christ's Presence

Meditation

To the elders among you, I appeal as a fellow elder, a witness of Christ's sufferings and one who also will share in the glory to be revealed: Be shepherds of God's flock that is under your care, serving as overseers—not because you must, but because you are willing, as God wants you to be; not greedy for money, but eager to serve; not lording it over those entrusted to you, but being examples to the flock. And when the Chief Shepherd appears, you will receive the crown of glory that will never fade away. Young men, in the same way be submissive to those who are older. All of you, clothe yourselves with humility toward one another, because, "God opposes the proud but gives grace to the humble." Humble yourselves, therefore, under God's mighty hand, that he may lift you up in due time (1 Peter 5:1-6).

PETER SPOKE from a unique perspective. He had personally witnessed Christ's suffering and glory (5:1). He was present at the Transfiguration and at the Ascension. Peter had watched Jesus' ministry, had looked into His face as He taught, and had lived with Him for three years. To Peter, Jesus was very real.

Here he says, "In light of Him—remembering how He ministered and suffered—this is how you should minister." His words impact not only pastors, but everyone in all areas of ministry. These words are relevant to our personal relationships as well.

The longer I serve the Lord, the more I feel the need to hear these truths again. They ring so true to experience.

Serving . . . not because you must, but because you are willing . . . not greedy for money, but eager to serve (v. 2).

It is easy to slip into doing "good" things for selfish reasons, even in the work of the church. But selfish motivation will eventually turn to bitterness and smallness.

All that changes when we perform every service for Christ himself. Ministry is then a work of love, and it is natural to be "willing" and "eager to serve."

Not lording it over those entrusted to you, but being examples to the flock (v. 3).

Lead by example, not by domination. This ties into the next point.

All of you, clothe yourselves with humility toward one another, because, "God opposes the proud but gives grace to the humble." Humble yourselves, therefore, under God's mighty hand (vv. 5-6).

Probably Christ's most unusual quality as a leader, as a King, as God himself, was His utter humility. When Isaiah looked ahead and saw the outlines of the coming Messiah, he described this quality:

He will not shout or cry out, or raise his voice in the streets. A bruised reed he will not break, and a smoldering wick he will not snuff out (Isaiah 42:2-3).

Jesus was so humble with the humble. He treated them as persons, as loved ones, as brothers and sisters. When we receive leadership responsibility, we tend to puff ourselves up as a way of commanding authority and getting our way. Peter's simple words are penetrating reminders.

They apply not only on the job and at church, but on the home front as well. As my three teenagers grow into independent adults, I'm learning the wisdom of this scriptural advice:

serve with a willing, unselfish spirit

lead by example

relate to them in humility, to the extent that I treat them respectfully as fellow human beings, not as people lower or less than myself

Lord, thank You for Your example. As I live before You, continue to teach me to serve others in Your Spirit.

❖

Acts of Love

Prayer Response

Lord, may
Your presence,
Your goodness,
Make every act
An act of love.